'Working in the world of finance, I com[...] very healthy bank balances but who [...] This book will be a real help to many [...] seeking a richer experience of life and a true relationship with God, and those who are currently blind to their true position. It is written in a clear and lucid style, is free from religious jargon and is very accessible. Full of illustrations, the authors unpack what it means to live in relationship with the living God and so to live life to the full. This is a great book to read for yourself and an excellent one to give to friends and colleagues.'

Simon Pilcher,
CHIEF EXECUTIVE, FIXED INCOME, M&G INVESTMENTS, LONDON

'Not a safe book. Peter Dickson is a bit sneaky (the book is so engagingly written) and yet terribly stubborn (he refuses to offer you a bland, smooth, mass-market, shrink-wrapped Jesus). So reading it may make you savingly angry or fearfully grateful-either of which will be okay. I find so refreshing this combination of contemporary clarity and old, rugged gospel.'

Dale Ralph Davis,
AUTHOR

'This is one of the best books of its kind that I have seen. It brings the familiar chapters of Luke's Gospel into the arena of the Twenty First Century, and makes the Christian faith real and relevant. One of the chapters is entitled "The Real Jesus". We encounter him throughout this whole book. I predict a wide use for it.'

Eric J. Alexander,
FORMERLY MINISTER ST GEORGE'S TRON, GLASGOW

'Peter Dickson has succeeded in transporting his readers from Aberdeen to the shores of Galilee in this vivid account of Dr Luke's impeccably researched biography of Jesus. But I must confess that this journey comes with a health warning – as we look at Jesus we'll discover much more about ourselves.'

Rico Tice,
AUTHOR, *CHRISTIANITY EXPLORED*

'Almost $100 billion is spent in the USA every year on medical research. Yet the humbling truth for all of us who sit across the desk from you in clinics and hospitals the world over, is that a scientific answer for the deeper sicknesses and troubles that we all experience will always be out of reach. But what if someone has the answer and it costs mankind nothing?

This book will steer you through the observations of a remarkable physician, Luke, who practised medicine 2000 years ago. It may have been long before antibiotics and scans, but he recognised and meticulously recorded the most significant event in world history. So whether you have never opened a Bible, or have one languishing on a shelf, I recommend you dust it off, take this book, and start a journey through the life of Jesus Christ. Using this book as a guide, you will learn to listen for what the Bible really says and come to see that it is anything but a quaint collection of tales.

This book will present you with a truly life-saving treatment – more than anything I or any other doctor can ever offer you!'

Simon Barker BSC (Hons) MD FRCSEd (Tr&Orth),
CONSULTANT ORTHOPAEDIC SURGEON, ROYAL ABERDEEN CHILDREN'S HOSPITAL

Rich

The reality of encountering Jesus

Peter Dickson
with David Gibson

CHRISTIAN
FOCUS

Peter Dickson has been minister at High Church, Hilton in Aberdeen since 1996. He grew up in Edinburgh and St. Andrews and became a Christian through the witness of Scripture Union camps. He is married to Eleanor, who comes from Inverness, and they have two children, Esther and Jamie.

David Gibson was born in America and grew up in East Africa and Northern Ireland. He has a Ph.D in Theology from the University of Aberdeen and is currently the Assistant Minister at High Church, Hilton. Married to Angela, his interests include writing, playing football, watching rugby, entertaining and being entertained by his children, Archie, Ella and Samuel.

You can find out more about their work by visiting:
www.highhilton.com

Scripture quotations taken from the *Holy Bible, New International Version*. Copyright © 1973, 1978, 1984 by International Bible Society. Used by permission of Hodder & Stoughton Publishers, a member of the Hodder Headline Group. All rights reserved. "NIV" is a registered trademark of International Bible Society. UK trademark number 1448790.

ISBN 978-1-84550-607-0

First published in 2010
by
Christian Focus Publications Ltd.,
Geanies House, Fearn, Tain, Ross-shire,
Scotland IV20 1TW, UK

Cover Design by Paul Lewis
Printed by Bell and Bain, Glasgow

Mixed Sources
Product group from well-managed
forests and other controlled sources
www.fsc.org Cert no. TT-COC-002769
© 1996 Forest Stewardship Council
FSC

Contents

Foreword

This book brings the Gospel of Luke, originally written in the first century, right into the experience of a twenty-first century audience. Luke's story is true on two levels. On the one hand, it is a historical account of what Jesus actually said and did and of the impact made by him on some of his contemporaries. On the other hand, it is a story that conveys a personal truth. This story did, and does, decisively change the lives of many who read it.

Luke wrote his Gospel in the manner of a historian and addressed it to a friend called Theophilus. In the same way, many modern authors dedicate their works to their friends although they expect them to be read by a much wider circle of people. Theophilus had heard what some of the early Christians were saying about Jesus but, as an educated man, he wanted to know whether what he had heard was true and reliable. Was Jesus indeed the Messiah or deliverer whose coming was prophesied in the Old Testament Scriptures? How could one know that the early preachers spoke the truth?

Luke's answer was to give a carefully researched historical account of the life of Jesus, showing that it gave the necessary foundation for what the preachers were saying. His book shows all the marks of being written by a competent author. He tells us that he went back to the people whose memories stretched back to the lifetime of Jesus. He says that he investigated things himself with great care. Where we can find independent evidence regarding the background to the story and the political events of the time, over and over again, Luke proves to be a reliable author. There were still many people around when he was writing who had memories of Jesus, whether through their own personal experience or through what had been handed down. These people would have known if the story that Luke told was false. In ancient society, great importance was attached to memories handed down by word of mouth and people would not get away with error or deceit. We have good reason to trust what Luke wrote, and also what his fellow-Christians wrote in the first books about Jesus.

The story of Jesus presented a challenge to those who heard it; his followers were persuaded by what he said and did. In particular the account of his death and resurrection convinced them that he was who he claimed to be, the person sent by God as the Saviour of the world and the final judge of all. Take Paul of Tarsus, for example, who underwent a conversion from savage hatred of the followers of Jesus to being a leading advocate for this new faith. In this way Luke's writing confronts us with life-changing truth. More than mere facts, the message about Jesus transmits new life and hope to those who believe it and live with Jesus as their Lord. What was true then has been confirmed by many subsequent readers right down to the present time.

Like the writers of this book, I and many others can testify to the living power of Jesus to change lives. From early on in life I believed the story of Jesus and his first followers and realised that it challenged me to make the vital decision whether I would acknowledge Jesus as my Saviour and Lord. I took that decision and I have never regretted it. It has made me a different person from what I would otherwise have been;

it has given purpose and direction to my life. Jesus has set me free from self-centredness to serve God and my fellow human beings, and given me grounds for believing that physical death is not the final end of life but the pathway to a future, better life in the presence of God. My prayer is that this book will help its readers by both creating and nourishing living faith in Jesus Christ.

Howard Marshall,
Emeritus Professor of New Testament,
University of Aberdeen

Preface

Sometimes a class of young children visits our church building as part of their school curriculum. As they arrive at the church door, all chatting cheerfully, the teacher invariably turns to quieten the children down. 'We are entering God's house, quiet now, you must be quiet.' The assumption, sincerely held I know, is that to be in the church building is the same as being close to God. There is the further assumption that God would, for whatever reason, object to hearing our voices.

Many people assume that to attend church must be the same as being close to God. To be involved in church *must* mean that we are involved in God's work. To be a leader of the church *must* mean that you are even closer to God than other church members. But the very opposite may be true. It is possible to be close to the church and far from God. It is possible, common even, to have all the outward trappings of Christian faith on display but not to have the heart of the Christian faith in place. If I walk into a bank because I hold an account there, make an appointment to speak to the manager and have a card that I can put in the ATM, that does not mean I have any money in the account. If my account remains empty then all the contact with the bank becomes somewhat meaningless. Similarly, were

I to visit your house for an evening that would not make it my home. Sitting at your table does not, in and of itself, make me part of your family. Something much more radical is required to make me belong.

My aim in writing this book is to explain what it means to belong to God. Being part of his family depends on one thing only: knowing Jesus Christ. I want to show why Jesus is the most important person who has ever lived and why encountering him is a matter of urgency.

Some who read these pages will be very familiar with church. I'm aware that others may have had little or no contact with Christianity. You might vaguely remember childhood involvement in church or some other religious activity, long since outgrown. Perhaps you have an occasional or formal interest in spiritual ideas. My assumption is that whoever we are, and whatever has happened to us in life, we share a common problem for which there is a surprising answer. I hope to show that what God gives us is not what we would ever dream of receiving. What God demands of us is not the kind of response we would ever expect him to desire.

Each section of the book is an attempt to explain a portion of Luke's Gospel. The relevant part of Luke is printed at the start of each chapter. What I have written will make most sense if you are able to take the time to read what Luke has written.

Acknowledgements

Writing this book has reminded me of my deep gratitude for the people who presented me with the claims of Jesus Christ. They led me to the rich experience of being forgiven by God. Others have since patiently taught me to appreciate the riches that come from knowing God. If this book achieves its simple aim of enabling people to encounter Jesus, then my gratitude for my mentors and friends will be greater still.

About five years ago Rico Tice suggested to me that a book, based on Luke's Gospel, would be valuable in helping others to hear the message of Jesus. I am grateful for his suggestion and for the enthusiasm with which it was offered which made the project seem realistic.

That this book ever became more than an idea is entirely due to the skill, patience, hard work and clarity of thought which David Gibson has brought to the task of it being written. I am very grateful for all the help he has given and for every other aspect of his involvement in our church family over the past six years.

A number of friends took the manuscript for a test drive and brought it back with excellent suggestions for improvement. I am indebted to Doug Easton for his sharp insight and detailed interaction with both the style and the content of the material. I also want to thank Simon Barker, Eleanor Dickson, Leonie Dryden, Jonathan and Jacqueline Gibson, David Humphris, Stuart Irvin, Will and Hannah Lind, Simon Pilcher, and Paul and Ruth Reed. Many of their comments have been incorporated and the book you now hold in your hands is much the better for them.

The church family at High Church, Hilton has been encouraging, appreciative and supportive for fourteen years as I have sought to help us listen to God speaking through the Bible. I have been very fortunate to serve people who have been patient with me, hungry for God's word and prayerful in their growing desire to bring others to know and love Jesus Christ. I dedicate this book to them with the hope that it may help us invite others to receive and treasure the generous grace of God.

1

A Rags to Riches Story

[14]Jesus returned to Galilee in the power of the Spirit, and news about him spread through the whole countryside. [15]He taught in their synagogues, and everyone praised him.

[16]He went to Nazareth, where he had been brought up, and on the Sabbath day he went into the synagogue, as was his custom. And he stood up to read. [17]The scroll of the prophet Isaiah was handed to him. Unrolling it, he found the place where it is written:

[18] The Spirit of the Lord is on me,
　　because he has anointed me
　　to preach good news to the poor.
He has sent me to proclaim freedom for the prisoners
　　and recovery of sight for the blind,
to release the oppressed,
　　[19]to proclaim the year of the Lord's favour.

[20]Then he rolled up the scroll, gave it back to the attendant and sat down. The eyes of everyone in the synagogue were fastened on him, [21]and he began by saying to them, 'Today this scripture is fulfilled in your hearing.'

[22]All spoke well of him and were amazed at the gracious words that came from his lips. 'Isn't this Joseph's son?' they asked.

Luke 4:14–22

The credit crunch

At the end of September 2008 the world went into financial
meltdown. You probably remember what happened (although,
if you're like me, perhaps you didn't understand much of what
the news reported). Suddenly, the expert chatter of accountants
and high-flying financiers filled the daily headlines. On
15 September, the first in a string of 'Manic Mondays', we saw
Lehman Brothers, one of the world's largest banks, collapse.
Within days, the UK government had nationalised mortgage
lender Bradford & Bingley; Lloyds TSB had agreed a £12bn
takeover of Britain's biggest mortgage lender, HBOS; and
regulators had closed down Washington Mutual, an American
bank with assets valued at £307bn.

Banks caught with bad investments now owed more than
they owned. The result was a frenetic global search for rescue
packages and bail-out schemes to restore market confidence
and financial stability. Shockwaves rippled round the world as
the US House of Representatives first rejected a £700bn rescue
plan for the US financial system, before finally accepting an
amended proposal. In Britain, politicians dashed between
Downing Street and various international destinations in
a desperate bid to prop up collapsing banks and stop the money
disappearing. On 8 October, *The Daily Telegraph*'s lead article
asked, 'Who will re-order today's world?' The crisis demanded
decisive action. The world needed someone to step in with the
insight, resolve, and ability to make a difference.

How did you feel when all this was happening? Some were
simply bewildered—after all, the bank account looked the same
and the cash machine still gave out new notes. Others were
genuinely fearful over job-security, agitated about the future,
anxious about a lifetime's savings put away for retirement or
for their grandchildren. Loss of control in situations like this
may soon create panic. We fear the loss of the world we know.
We wonder if anyone can bail us out of the mess.

A rescue mission

It might come as a surprise to you, but the Bible describes Jesus as the ultimate solution to the worst credit crisis the world has ever known.

The passage from Luke's Gospel printed at the start of this chapter reveals the reality of the global crisis described in the Bible. These verses recount an incident right at the start of Jesus' public life. It is the announcement of his manifesto: a crucial statement of what he is all about and what he has come to do.

Jesus has returned to his home town of Nazareth. Back in the familiar surroundings of his childhood, he delivers the Sabbath sermon in the synagogue. Expectations were high; we're told that wherever else Jesus had preached 'everyone praised him'. The atmosphere was electric. This promised to be a memorable sermon: 'the eyes of everyone in the synagogue were fastened on him'. And when he's finished, Jesus is clearly the leading contender in *The Times* 'Preacher of the Year' competition. The entire congregation is astonished at the 'gracious words' that fall from his lips. I have only once preached in my home congregation in St. Andrews, Scotland, and the reaction to my sermon was mild and innocuous at best. That's probably how most people react to most sermons. On the scale of relevance, preaching often registers somewhere between mind-numbingly dull and dreadfully disappointing.

Maybe the reaction Jesus received was because his sermon was so short! Actually, it wasn't that at all. It was because Jesus read one of the most amazing promises of rescue in the Old Testament, and then claimed to be the rescuer whom Isaiah described: 'Today, this scripture is fulfilled in your hearing.' In the book of Isaiah, God had promised 'good news to the poor, freedom for the prisoners, sight for the blind, and release for those oppressed', and Jesus says, 'I am the one who will do it. That is what I am here to do.' How are we to understand this mission statement of Jesus? Who are the poor, the prisoners, the blind and the oppressed that Jesus has come to help?

You will find the poor in London, Paris, or New York, although some of them may seem rich compared to those living in third world shanty towns. Countless thousands in India, the Philippines, and the vast cities of Latin America or Africa, live on virtually nothing and die every day from preventable disease or malnutrition. If Jesus had these poor people in mind, and his good news was the alleviation of their poverty, he clearly embarked on an unsuccessful mission. Indeed, as we read on in Luke's Gospel we discover a curious fact. After saying that he has come to preach good news to the poor, we often find Jesus in the homes of the wealthy. Luke seems to go out of his way to show Jesus fraternising with the rich.

What about freedom for the prisoners? This claim could leave us scratching our heads when we know that Jesus' own relative, John the Baptist, languished in a prison cell before King Herod had John's head lopped off as a present for one of the pretty dancers at his birthday party. Rather macabre after-dinner entertainment we may think; but did Jesus simply not get there in time? Either that, and he failed in his mission, or Luke intends us to see something more in what Jesus said he came to do.

Next, consider the blind. Jesus says that they are to receive their sight, which would be good news indeed. Of course Jesus gave eyesight to some blind people. There are, however, millions of blind people in the world today who would perhaps be sceptical about Jesus' claim to be a preacher of good news to them.

When it comes to the oppressed, many regimes ignore every human rights clause in the book. They subject people to conditions that should not be permitted for animals, and the dignity of justice (political, social, and every other kind) seems a mere pipe dream.

Please do not misunderstand me. The needs of the economically poor and the physically oppressed are high on God's agenda for this world. It's just that people often mistake these matters for the core of Jesus' message. So what does Jesus mean by talking in this way?

God's favour and my debt

The key to understanding what Jesus came to do is found in the short summary statement of his purpose, which is easy to miss. It appears at the end of what he read out in the synagogue that day: 'To proclaim the year of the Lord's favour'. That phrase encapsulates all that has just come before it, and sheds further light on each of the things that Jesus will do.

Think back to the Jubilee Campaign which was so prominent in the year 2000. 'The year of the Lord's favour' is a phrase rooted in the Old Testament idea of a Jubilee year. Among the people of Israel, God established the practice that every seven years there would be a Jubilee year when everyone's debts would be wiped out and their property returned. All the slaves would be set free. God's people would have a clean start. A Jubilee year. A year of favour. Jesus says: 'I have come to proclaim the favour of God to everyone who owes him a debt. I have come to end the spiritual credit crisis that has left you destitute and bankrupt, and which you are powerless to sort out.'

No one likes being in debt. Some of you reading these pages take great pride in the thought that you have always worked for what you have, and you have waited before buying the things you want so that you would never be in debt. It's horrible to be in serious debt. Jesus is saying, 'I have come to create the ultimate headline: "Good news, Good news! Listen – all debts can now be cancelled. You can have a clean start with God. He is going to cancel everything that you owe to him. This is the time of God's favour."'

This announcement may raise a real question for us: in what sense am I in debt to God? You may be familiar with the words of the Lord's Prayer, 'Forgive us our debts, as we forgive our debtors'. In the Bible, 'debts' is a common way of describing 'sins'—the things we do that separate us from God and twist our relationships with one another out of shape. By calling our sins 'debts', the Bible is creating an image drawn from the real world we inhabit to help us understand exactly what it means to be in the wrong. We may borrow money from the bank, or from a friend, and therefore be in debt; so too the reality is that we are in debt to God. We are in debt because of who God is, and because of who we are and what we have done. We might work all our lives to avoid debt to banks or credit cards, yet all the while we have a massive debt in our spiritual bank account with the God who gave us life.

According to the Bible, because God is our creator, we owe him everything. He loves us and therefore sustains our lives and provides us with everything we need to live for his glory. Tragically, however, we have squandered our God-given privileges and resources, creating a dire situation of insolvency. We owe God everything but have no way of paying back anything.

Picture a student who has irresponsibly forgotten to organise accommodation for the new academic year. Fortunately, his aunt lives in town and offers him a room for nothing. She cooks his meals, does his laundry and irons his clothes, yet six months later she has not received one word of thanks for all she has done. When we see someone take and relish a gift with no appreciation for the giver, we think, 'That person is ungrateful and selfish.' When someone gives something to someone else, at the very least it creates the debt of gratitude. The Bible says that every human being is like that student with free accommodation: a life of overflowing gratitude is a debt we owe to God, but which we have not paid. We have enjoyed God's good gifts without pausing to adore him for them. We have lived in his world without giving him the worship of our hearts; we have lived as if he is not even there. Truth be told, even when we hear that God is there, we don't want him (or anyone else) ruling our lives. We'd rather God was out of the way so we could have his job.

To live with ingratitude, ignoring God, whilst making ourselves rulers of our own lives means that we create for ourselves a spiritual credit crisis. We are in the red with God. We owe him. Just like a lender might send a letter to say 'Full payment is now due', much like a library might send a note to recall an overdue book, if God were to call time on the life he gave us and in which we have ignored him, what could we use to pay him back?

Many of us instinctively want to point to the good things we have done, the kind of things we hope might just haul us out of the spiritual red into the black and tip the scales in our favour. We imagine that we would be able to offer God the gold of loyal service to others, maybe even service in his church! We come with the silver and bronze of careers which have been publicly recognised. We approach God with the currency of children who have turned out to be responsible citizens. But the problem with even the best that we can bring is that it is like offering the bank a handful of copper coins to repay a £1m mortgage. It is Jesus who came to help us see our bankruptcy.

Most of us feel uncomfortable when asked to consider our genuine spiritual need with honesty. The truth is that our debt problem is so bad that we cannot solve it ourselves. We need a bail-out package—a rescue plan. We need someone to write off our bad debt; to deal with our toxic assets. If we think that we can be good enough for God, then what we fail to see is that how good we think we are depends on who we compare ourselves to. Compare yourself to Hitler, or Stalin, or the guy on the front page of the *Evening Express* who set fire to a block of flats and you will come up smelling of roses. But what if you compare yourself to Mother Theresa? What if God only accepts into his kingdom people who are that good? Worse still, what if we compare ourselves to God himself—what kind of goodness would be good enough for a perfect God? The reality is that there will never be enough credit to overcome our debt. We need our debt cancelled. We need it written off. Paid for and taken away forever by someone else. But who?

When Jesus stood in the synagogue that day what he was saying was this: 'I have come to cancel what you owe to God. However much you are trapped in the poverty of a totally self-absorbed life, however blind you have been to God's fatherly love and care for you, however imprisoned you are in a sin-mangled life, I can give you a fresh start with God.' Trying to pay off our debt to God ourselves is an impossible burden. It cannot be done. What we need is grace: someone to do for us what we cannot do ourselves. Jesus came to release us from the agony and grim toil of trying to earn what cannot be earned.

Luke's Gospel and this book

As we begin to take in what Luke tells us about Jesus, let me be honest with you. So far I have only given you half the story of Luke 4. We have left Jesus with his congregation in raptures at his preaching, but by the end of the chapter the same people are so furious with him that they try to murder him by throwing him off a cliff. Things turned ugly that day in Nazareth, and it was all because Jesus realised that his listeners hadn't understood a word he had said. They are poor, but think they are rich; blind, but think they can see; enslaved, but think they are free. So instead of words of grace for them, now Jesus only has words of judgment. They embark on a rejection of Jesus that will seal Jesus' rejection of them. This shows that encountering Jesus is a hazardous business. There is no neutral position to occupy once he has addressed us. Either we hear what he says and believe him, or even our indifference and our apathy counts as a rejection of him. In the final chapter we will come back to this second half of Luke 4 to see exactly what turned a polite congregation into a mob baying for Jesus' blood.

But before we get to that last chapter, we will explore how Jesus brings wealth instead of poverty, sight instead of blindness, and freedom for those in captivity. That's what makes up the main body of this book: different facets of the greatest bail-out the world will ever see. We won't be able to look at everything that Luke has written, so I have gathered some of the main examples of where we see Jesus rescuing the lost. We will focus in on Jesus as the one who can take us from the rags of spiritual bankruptcy to the unimaginable riches of all our debts being wiped out. Along the way we will ask:

Why does Luke think that Jesus can make us rich?
What is this wealth we should want more than anything else in the world?
What do we have to do to get it?

In chapter nine we will return to the second part of Luke 4 so that we have the chance to see what the Nazareth congregation was unwilling to see. In other words, as we see Jesus announce God's solution to our true poverty, my hope is that you will see—just like me—that you are one of the poor, one of the blind, one of the oppressed, one of the needy. These chapters explain that Jesus brings the best news I have ever heard, and I have tried to write them in such a way that they offer you the real meaning of Luke's Gospel, which is the best news you will ever read.

Why should we believe Luke?

There's one more thing to consider at the outset: how can we trust what Luke has to say to us about Jesus? For many people, turning to the pages of the Bible to read about someone who lived two thousand years ago is similar to reading a bed-time story to children, which begins, 'Once upon a time...'. Those opening words of any fairy tale are the give-away that what you're about to read is make-believe. Magical, wonderful, mysterious, but certainly not true. When we turn to the opening pages of Luke's Gospel we read about an angel appearing to an old man, a virgin conceiving a child, and then shepherds on a hillside catching sight of thousands of angels in the sky. If we're honest, it might seem more sensible to admit that we're in the realm of the fairy-tale. All great stuff for the nativity play, but that's where it belongs. No firm basis in reality, either in history or in our twenty-first-century lives.

There is one problem with this viewpoint. Luke does not begin his Gospel with miraculous events but with a sober-minded explanation of what he is doing. Consider the first words he wrote:

> [1] Many have undertaken to draw up an account of the things that have been fulfilled among us, [2] just as they were handed down to us by those who from the first were eyewitnesses and servants of the word. [3] Therefore, since I myself have carefully investigated everything from the beginning, it seemed good also to me to write an orderly account for you, most excellent Theophilus, [4] so that you may know the certainty of the things you have been taught.
>
> *Luke 1:1–4*

We can't be completely sure who Theophilus was, but his appearance here at the start of Luke's Gospel means that Luke wrote with a clear purpose in mind. He wanted to provide his friend with the kind of orderly account that would help Theophilus be certain of what he had been told about Jesus. Luke's aim is to give us a reliable, truthful, historically accurate portrait. When we see his aim clearly then the weird and wonderful events with which he starts his account (angels, a virgin birth, shepherds and the like) take on a historical rather than fictitious character.

Take the shepherds, for example. Luke tells us that an angel announced to them that a Saviour had been born, and that this angel was then joined by a whole host of angels who were praising God (Luke 2:8–13). If Luke was trying to make the miraculous sound remotely plausible then shepherds are the last people he would have picked for the task. Shepherds were not recognised for their hard work or skill. They were the lowest form of human life in their day, men who were fit for nothing else, and the last to be considered worthy of receiving important news.

Whenever we hear news, we usually want to find out if it comes from a reliable source. If the workplace gossip stops you in the corridor and passes on some tasty titbit of information that he heard in the staffroom then you are wise to listen to it with caution. But if your solicitor phones you with some news then you are going to pay a bit more attention. No one in their right mind would invent a tale being announced to shepherds, not if they wanted people to take it seriously. Unless, of course, it was true. Unless you had to record that it was announced to shepherds because that's what happened.

But there is even more to it than this. The fact that angels appeared to shepherds is part of a recurring pattern in the opening pages of Luke's story. It ties in closely with the main thrust of Jesus' mission. He has come for the very people we might least expect him to care about. The historical details of Luke's narrative aren't just there to convince our minds; they are there to humble our hearts. They are there to show us that Jesus has come for people in debt, people like us—if we are willing to see that we need him.

2

God in the Dock

²⁶In the sixth month, God sent the angel Gabriel to Nazareth, a town in Galilee, ²⁷to a virgin pledged to be married to a man named Joseph, a descendant of David. The virgin's name was Mary. ²⁸The angel went to her and said, 'Greetings, you who are highly favoured! The Lord is with you.'

²⁹Mary was greatly troubled at his words and wondered what kind of greeting this might be. ³⁰But the angel said to her, 'Do not be afraid, Mary, you have found favour with God. ³¹You will be with child and give birth to a son, and you are to give him the name Jesus. ³²He will be great and will be called the Son of the Most High. The Lord God will give him the throne of his father David, ³³and he will reign over the house of Jacob forever; his kingdom will never end.'

³⁴ 'How will this be,' Mary asked the angel, 'since I am a virgin?'

³⁵The angel answered, 'The Holy Spirit will come upon you, and the power of the Most High will overshadow you. So the holy one to be born will be called the Son of God.'

Luke 1:26-35

¹In those days Caesar Augustus issued a decree that a census should be taken of the entire Roman world. ²(This was the first census that took place while Quirinius was governor of Syria.) ³And everyone went to his own town to register.

⁴So Joseph also went up from the town of Nazareth in Galilee to Judea, to Bethlehem the town of David, because he belonged to the house and line of David. ⁵He went there to register with Mary, who was pledged to be married to him and was expecting a child. ⁶While they were there, the time came for the baby to be born, ⁷and she gave birth to her firstborn, a son. She wrapped him in cloths and placed him in a manger, because there was no room for them in the inn.

⁸And there were shepherds living out in the fields nearby, keeping watch over their flocks at night. ⁹An angel of the Lord appeared to them, and the glory of the Lord shone around them, and they were terrified. ¹⁰But the angel said to them, 'Do not be afraid. I bring you good news of great joy that will be for all the people. ¹¹Today in the town of David a Saviour has been born to you; he is Christ the Lord. ¹²This will be a sign to you: You will find a baby wrapped in cloths and lying in a manger.'

¹³Suddenly a great company of the heavenly host appeared with the angel, praising God and saying,

¹⁴'Glory to God in the highest,
   and on earth peace to men on whom his favour rests.'

¹⁵When the angels had left them and gone into heaven, the shepherds said to one another, 'Let's go to Bethlehem and see this thing that has happened, which the Lord has told us about.'

Luke 2:1-15

Turning the tables

> The ancient man approached God (or even the gods) as the accused person approaches his judge. For the modern man the roles are reversed. He is the judge: God is in the dock. He is quite a kindly judge: if God should have a reasonable defence for being the god who permits war, poverty and disease, he is ready to listen to it. The trial may even end in God's acquittal. But the important thing is that Man is on the bench and God is in the dock.

C. S. Lewis, who wrote those words, was correct: most of us decide for ourselves whether God deserves our respect or even our attention.

The complaints arrayed against God boil down to two kinds. On the one hand, God is too distant and detached; too impersonal. We therefore conclude that he is not accessible or near to us. On the other hand, God is too demanding of us and expects too much from us; his standards are too high and he does not love us as we are.

A recent dramatisation took up these issues by portraying a group of Jewish men in a concentration camp, facing death in the gas chamber. The night before their extermination they decide to put God on trial for what he has done. In a moving drama, they agree that God is to blame for what has happened. He has let them down at the point where they needed him most. God is remote in the hour of their greatest need, and his love for them as his chosen people is thrown into doubt because of his absence.

This drama is powerful because very little of it is made up. The questions it raises aren't just asked by philosophers and theologians in the comfort of academia's cloisters; they are the questions you and I ask as we live in a world which often doesn't make sense to us. Crisis may enter our lives in the form of unemployment, marital breakdown, bereavement or betrayal. When it hurts the most, what we want to know is: if there's a God, where is he and why doesn't he do something?

Luke's Gospel makes the startling claim that in Jesus Christ, God has come down to us. He stepped into our world and stooped down to where we are. God is not remote or absent or unloving; he is present. Jesus lived in our world for over thirty years. He had an address, he drank wine and ate food and, most significantly, he knows all about our pain.

Some years ago, when he was President of the United States, George Bush flew in to Iraq on Thanksgiving Day to be with the armed forces of his country. He knew it would be effective in all sorts of ways to go there and be with them. A boost to morale, a publicity manoeuvre that proclaimed, 'We can win and I'm right there with you.' A visit like that is strategic, but it is also fleeting. It is wonderful to have your Commander-in-Chief with you for an evening, but he will not be with you in the morning. Precisely because he is the most important person in America, he will not be on the front-line as bullets whistle through the air. He will be long gone, whisked away in the safety of his armoured vehicle or military helicopter.

When Jesus was born, God came to be with his people. But it was no furtive or fleeting presidential visit. Rather, the Son of God became a human being and came into our world as the king whom God had always promised to send. He came to be the rescuer, to take the bullets, to bail out the troops when victory was no longer possible. This deliverance, planned by the God who made the world, was not passed down the chain of command for someone else to carry out. He came himself. Jesus was born.

They say that at eight days old it is sometimes possible to predict a child's personality and character. Perhaps it is the doting grandmother or the overwhelmed new father who has studied this little bundle of joy and is confident they know what wee Jimmy is going to be like. 'Oh what a laid back fellow

he is—just like his father.' 'Oh what a demanding little thing
you are—just like...'

We know the kind of conversation and, of course, it's mostly
nonsense. The truth is we have no idea what direction a person's
life and personality and circumstances will take. Nor can we
disentangle that potent combination of nature and nurture
because, from birth, they are intertwined and inseparable. And,
really, we don't need to know.

So it is remarkable to discover that again and again in the
Bible when a significant child is born God tells people in
advance exactly what is going to happen and what the child
is going to do. God does this to show us that he is organising
his world and people. To help us recognise him and know him,
God has recorded in the Bible several instances where he says in
advance what is going to happen. Then, when it does, everyone
can say, 'Oh, this is just as the prophet said. We knew to expect
this.'

Of the many examples of this in the Bible the most
significant is the birth of Jesus. His arrival would probably
have gone unnoticed had it not been accompanied by so many
words from God explaining what was going on. Take a look
at the first three chapters of Luke. Announcements from God
seemed two-a-penny in those days: angels and prophets and
priests; Mary and Joseph receiving a much needed explanation;
a star so striking that it couldn't be missed; and even the birth
of another baby who would serve as a messenger about Jesus.

The birth of Jesus is surrounded by words and explanations.
There are so many we can't miss them. Except—we do miss
them. In many schools the nativity play does not contain
a single sentence of explanation about who Jesus is or why he
came into the world. That gives the impression that the point
of these incredible events was so that we could have donkeys
on a stage and tea-towels on the heads of little shepherds while
two lucky children get to be Mary and Joseph. Luke says to us—

don't just look. Listen! Listen to what God is saying because it is only his words of explanation that make sense of what is happening.

We will look at three different aspects of Luke's description of Jesus' birth. First, we will look at words spoken to Mary, which declare that Jesus will be a king who reigns forever. Secondly, we will notice the details of Jesus' birth, which reveal that Jesus is a king who serves. Thirdly, in the words that the angel speaks to the shepherds we will see that Jesus is a king who can save us, whatever our situation. Luke thus gives us a three-fold explanation of what this incredible birth means. Each aspect says something astonishing about Jesus.

The king who reigns forever

The angel tells Mary that the child she carries will be an eternal king, rather than a temporary one. Her son will be given 'the throne of his father David'. Like any child born into a royal family with a claim to the throne, Jesus is born in Israel's royal line, the family of David, and therefore the throne belongs to him. But that isn't all. Not only is Jesus the king, but he will be king forever: 'The Lord God will give him the throne of his father David, and he will reign over the house of Jacob forever; his kingdom will never end.' There is no-one to come after him. No next-in-line. He will never abdicate; there will be no more coronations. Jesus is king forever.

I don't know any ordinary human being who will live forever. Some people seem to have been around forever. Terry Wogan has been on the BBC since broadcasting began. Paolo Maldini played left-back for Italy since the game of football was invented. We know what it's like to have people in the world who seem to go on and on and who always seem to be there. And yet, of course, we know that they won't be. One day they will die. No-one will remember Wogan in fifty years and Maldini's knees eventually wore out. If you've never heard of either of them then that probably proves my point. Jesus is no ordinary child because he is a king forever (not just temporarily, like every other king). These words of the angel explain that he is not a mere human being. Somehow, with more mystery than we can ever comprehend, here is the eternal God coming to be born on earth and to reign as king in a way that will never end.

This sheds some light on the objections of distance and indifference on God's part that we aired at the start of the chapter. The Christian faith will not help you if you want to raise questions about God in the abstract. The gospel will not help if you want to talk about where God is, but you do not want to talk about Jesus. The Christian faith will not answer your questions about what God is up to, or why he is not doing what you think he should be doing, if you do not want to talk about Jesus. There is no Christian view of God that does not recognise that we can only talk about God meaningfully if we talk about Jesus. If we talk about Christianity, and in the same breath talk about a detached or distant God, then we are talking about two different things. For the meaning of the angel's words to Mary is not just that God has come near to us, but that God has become one of us. You can't get nearer than that.

That in itself is incredible. But if it's true, how would you expect God to behave when he entered our world?

The king who serves us himself

Think now of the second objection—that God is too demanding of us—and notice some of the details at the start of Luke 2. We have the historical details which announce when all of this happened: 'In those days Caesar Augustus issued a decree that a census should be taken of the entire Roman world. (This was the first census that took place while Quirinius was governor of Syria.) And everyone went to his own town to register' (Luke 2:1-2). It's the kind of detail that could make our eyes glaze over as we skim on to the more interesting bit about a baby being born. But Luke wants us to see that God arrived in the world during a census: he came when the events would be documented. Here is God himself stepping into the real world at a specific moment in history and in a particular place.

More than this, however, there are practical details which explain the extraordinary significance of what is happening. 'While they were there (in Bethlehem) the time came for the baby to be born, and she gave birth to her firstborn, a son. She wrapped him in cloths and placed him in a manger, because there was no room for them in the inn' (Luke 2:6–7). We're so used to this from hearing the Christmas story that we miss how staggering it is because of what Mary has been told. Her son will be called 'the Son of the Most High. The Lord God will give him the throne of his father David, and he will reign over the house of Jacob forever; his kingdom will never end' (Luke 1:32–33). If we're reading carefully we will do a double-take and read again. The birth of an eternal king who will rule forever, the Son of God, in an animal's feeding trough?

Ponder what these details show us about Jesus. He is a king—but he does not come to a throne in a blaze of dazzling glory. He comes to a place where there is no room for him. He lies among the animals. The amazing thing about the birth of Jesus Christ is not just that here is the supposedly distant God stepping into the world to be near us. More amazing than that, here is the supposedly demanding and insensitive God, stooping down to serve us, not coming to make demands of us.

A friend of mine visited Thailand and was taken to visit an expensive shrine that housed the local god. All around the deity on the floor were gifts of money and food brought to him by his devotees. My friend was struck by the fact that the god sat there in comfort while the worshippers lived in abject poverty, desperately hoping that if they did enough to please him then things might get better. The good news in Luke's Gospel is that God acts differently. He has abolished religious pretence because when he comes into the world he does not come to live in an expensive shrine (or church!) to be served by people who are trying to impress him. Instead, Jesus is born in a smelly outhouse because he has come to serve those who want nothing to do with him. It is an amazing contrast. It takes a lifetime to get the dynamic of what God has done into our thinking; it seems so strange that we can hardly believe it. That Almighty God should come down from heaven, and before he ever asks us to do anything for him, he insists that he must first serve us. He must stoop low and be born in a manger because that's what we need him to do.

One of my colleagues went to Malawi recently. Wherever he went, after being introduced to the people, the women would come and kneel in front of him. And of course he was thinking, 'No, no, no, you don't need to do that! You don't need to serve me. It's not right.'

It's tempting, isn't it, to think of us needing to be served as nonsense. 'How bizarre to think that I need God to serve me or to save me. I am fine without him; I am self-sufficient and competent. I could lend God a hand, and I know his poor old church is always needing people and money. I could certainly do a bit for God, but to think that he could do anything for me! No, God, you don't need to do that! I have everything money can buy and I am protected by insurance policies and pension schemes. I think you had better serve other people, Lord Jesus, but I really don't think you need to serve me (unless, of course, a crisis comes my way which I can't control. In which case I will get in touch).'

Luke says to us, keep reading my account of Jesus Christ and observe what he does. Listen to what he says as he makes people rich, sets them free and gives them sight by serving them. Be careful to understand that he wants to serve you in a particular way. He wants to serve you by placing himself in the dock. For the birth of the Lord Jesus Christ in a stable (when the local hospital may seem more appropriate) is just the beginning of his stooping low to serve and to rescue the lost outcasts of this world like you and me. It is a journey that will take him from the manger to the cross. The supposedly distant God steps into the world. The supposedly demanding God bends low, not just to serve me, but even to stand in the dock instead of me.

The king who saves us—whoever we are

By the time we've read the opening chapters of Luke's Gospel we have met an assortment of people. We've read about angels appearing to old men, young women, and the rough-and-ready shepherds on a hillside. There is significance in all these details because they show us the kind of people that the king of the universe wants to be with when he enters the world. Wouldn't we normally expect a great king to be with the rich and famous and to be right at home in celebrity culture? But when Jesus entered our world, the people he came to be with included those who in the first-century belonged in the category of the 'poor'. People whom society didn't take seriously or have much time for. Luke is making a deliberate point. God is not just interested in the people who are normally regarded as worthy and attractive. After the angel announces to Mary that she will give birth to Jesus, Mary cries out in praise to God:

> [49]For the Mighty One has done great things for me—holy is his name. [50]His mercy extends to those who fear him, from generation to generation. [51]He has performed mighty deeds with his arm; he has scattered those who are proud in their inmost thoughts. [52]He has brought down rulers from their thrones but has lifted up the humble. [53]He has filled the hungry with good things but has sent the rich away empty.

Luke 1:49–53

The words of Mary's song are a beautiful summary of Jesus' own mission. Jesus has come for the humble, the outcast, the hungry, the weak. He has come for people who cannot help themselves. He has come to rescue them. He has come as their Saviour. This is exactly what the angel told the shepherds on the hillside: 'Do not be afraid. I bring you good news of great joy that will be for all the people. Today in the town of David a Saviour has been born to you; he is Christ the Lord' (Luke 2:10-11). Why should a message about a saviour be announced to shepherds? The shepherds, you remember from chapter one, were ill thought of according to the social ranking of the day. This means that there is no one so bad, so irrelevant in the eyes of the world, so unreliable, so sinful and looked down upon that they are unworthy to receive this message. That is why the angel says this message is 'for all the people'.

Some of us find the idea of God helping certain people hard to swallow. We think what they have done puts them so far beyond the pale that the thought of Jesus coming for them is an outrage and an offence. They are too bad and do not deserve forgiveness.

On the other hand, for many of us it is not other people who seem unworthy of the good news. Sometimes we are our own worst critics. We don't need other people to tell us that we are unworthy of God's love because we tell ourselves that every day. And some of our own harsh self-assessment may be true. But listen again to the angel. This news is for everyone regardless of what they have done. This news is for you regardless of what anyone says about you and regardless of what you think of yourself.

We can be slippery characters when the God who loves us wants to address us directly. When God tells us that he loves us we hang our heads in shame and say, 'Oh, I'm not worthy of God's love'. When God says 'I want to speak to you about your sin problem', we deny there is a problem at all. When God wants to lift us up, we put ourselves down. When God's word speaks honestly about what is wrong with us, we stick our heads firmly in the sand. How direct the angel was when he spoke to the shepherds: 'I bring you good news of great joy—a Saviour has been born to you.' To you shepherds. The facts are true. It really happened. But better still the message conveyed by the facts is also true—Jesus came as the Saviour for all types of people.

In the passages from Luke printed at the start of this chapter there is a word that appears three times: 'favour'. Mary is told twice that God's favour has come to her; the shepherds hear that God's favour is now shown to the earth. We met this word in chapter one when Jesus burst onto the scene. He said he had come 'To proclaim the year of the Lord's favour'. The end of all debts; the ultimate bail-out. The best fresh start in the world. Now we can see that Jesus is repeating exactly what God had said about him when he was born. He is the king and so he is powerful enough to do what he says. He is the servant king and so he will bend down to lift the fallen. He is the saviour king and so he will set his people free. God has come near to us in Jesus.

3

The Real Jesus

Then he went down to Capernaum, a town in Galilee, and on the Sabbath began to teach the people. ³²They were amazed at his teaching, because his message had authority.

³³ In the synagogue there was a man possessed by a demon, an evil spirit. He cried out at the top of his voice, ³⁴'Ha! What do you want with us, Jesus of Nazareth? Have you come to destroy us? I know who you are—the Holy One of God!'

³⁵'Be quiet!' Jesus said sternly. 'Come out of him!' Then the demon threw the man down before them all and came out without injuring him.

³⁶All the people were amazed and said to each other, 'What is this teaching? With authority and power he gives orders to evil spirits and they come out!' ³⁷And the news about him spread throughout the surrounding area.

³⁸Jesus left the synagogue and went to the home of Simon. Now Simon's mother-in-law was suffering from a high fever, and they asked Jesus to help her. ³⁹So he bent over her and rebuked the fever, and it left her. She got up at once and began to wait on them.

⁴⁰When the sun was setting, the people brought to Jesus all who had various kinds of sickness, and laying his hands on each one, he healed them. ⁴¹Moreover, demons came out of many people, shouting, 'You are the Son of God!' But he rebuked them and would not allow them to speak, because they knew he was the Christ.

⁴²At daybreak Jesus went out to a solitary place. The people were looking for him and when they came to where he was, they tried to keep him from leaving them. ⁴³But he said, 'I must preach the good news of the kingdom of God to the other towns also, because that is why I was sent.' ⁴⁴And he kept on preaching in the synagogues of Judea.

Luke 4:31–44

The real deal

Now and then a story about Jesus makes it into the news. Recent documentaries have alleged we now have evidence that Jesus didn't rise from the dead or, more dramatically, that he didn't die but got married instead. Such stories range from the far-fetched to the fair-minded, depending on how the historical evidence about Jesus is probed. But you may also have seen in your newspaper, or online, claims about Jesus that come straight from the realm of *Alice in Wonderland*. In November 2006 the Metro newspaper in London reported that the image of Jesus was visible in the fur of a terrier dog called Angus MacDougall. The list is endless: Jesus has appeared in spilled hot chocolate, a door in IKEA Glasgow, and in images of dental x-rays, to name a few.

I don't think that many people take the extreme Jesus stories seriously, but I do know that we sometimes get into an extraordinary muddle over who Jesus is. Confusion usually reigns when people play the 'I think' game: 'I think Jesus was a prophet', or 'I like to think Jesus was a great moral teacher.' 'In my opinion Jesus was a misguided, lonely man'. The tragedy is that so many of us give more credence to popular stories and our own thoughts about Jesus than we do to the Bible's portrayal of him.

In this passage Luke gives us three portraits of Jesus to clear up any muddle. Jesus is a deliverer; he is a healer; and he is a preacher. The passage follows immediately from the section of Luke that we looked at in chapter one. Here we have Jesus beginning to do all that he had said he would do in Luke 4:16-30. Just as he promised, Jesus now turns to the marginalised in his society. As we see Jesus with the demonised and the diseased, ministering to women, and to men, Luke shows us the prisoners being set free, the blind being given sight, the poor being made rich. The Jesus we meet as events unfold is not always the Jesus we expect to find.

Jesus the deliverer—his absolute authority

As in Nazareth, so now in Capernaum, people are amazed at the authority of Jesus' words. But this is not the only reaction to Jesus. The agonising cry of a demon-possessed man interrupts the atmosphere of astonished listening. Jesus has not addressed him directly, but he cries out as he hears Jesus' teaching. We are about to see that people who at first liked Jesus' teaching do not have a clue who he really is. But an evil spirit cries out, 'I know who you are—the Holy One of God.' The unseen spiritual world has a clearer grasp of the real Jesus than the people praising his teaching. There is no muddle here. Satan knows who Jesus is and what he is about.

In the middle of the last century it was common in scholarly circles to argue that Jesus' hearers were uneducated and that 'demon possession' would, in our progressive age, be understood as severe mental illness or epilepsy. There are two main problems with this argument. First, it rides rough-shod over the text. In the rest of our passage Luke, a physician, makes clear that people in the ancient world knew the difference between illness and demon-possession; they did not always equate one with the other. Jesus heals some people without any mention of evil spirits being present. This argument is a form of modern cultural arrogance and it is closely connected to the second problem. Many scholars who expressed doubts about the reality of demon possession in Jesus' culture were simply reflecting a viewpoint of modern Western thinking. But now that the Christian faith has spread significantly round the world, an incident like this in the ministry of Jesus does not even raise an eyebrow among an overwhelming number of Bible readers in places and cultures where the presence of spiritual forces of evil is a recognised reality. When we stand back from our own narrow view of the world and look again at what Luke says, there are no compelling reasons to think that he is not telling the truth: here in the synagogue Jesus was face to face with the evil world of spiritual darkness and its effect in one broken human life.

For this man, Jesus' rebuke of the evil spirit would have meant the end of a miserable existence blighted by uncontrollable actions and confusion. The man discovers a new-found ability to hear Jesus' words with heartfelt appreciation, free from fear. The demon is terrified: 'What do you want with us, Jesus of Nazareth? Have you come to destroy us?' Interestingly, although there is only one evil spirit, it refers twice to 'us'. Perhaps the demon is speaking of the man and the demon as 'us'. If this were true, then the demon assumes that for Jesus to destroy it would also destroy the man. If so, Jesus' authority is such that he can rebuke the demon and leave the man unharmed. It is more likely, however, that in speaking of 'us' the demon realises that the ministry of Jesus is an onslaught not just against one solitary demon, but against all the forces of evil. The demon sees that this is just the beginning. Its destruction is beckoning; but so too is the complete overthrow of all the forces of spiritual evil.

This is a profound insight into something that the rest of the Bible makes clear. The apostle John writes that 'The reason the Son of God appeared was to destroy the devil's work'

(1 John 3:8). Hebrews 2:14 tells us Jesus came so that 'he might destroy him who holds the power of death—that is, the devil—and free those who all their lives were held in slavery by their fear of death.' The biblical view of our bankruptcy and poverty is that Jesus came to bring freedom because every normal, sane, decent and upright person who does not see who Jesus is and what he came to do is living in 'the kingdom of darkness' (Col. 1:13), enslaved to the devil's spiritual forces of evil (Eph. 2:1-2; 2 Cor. 4:1-3). That might sound like we're back with *Alice in Wonderland*, but let's pause to think more about this by looking at a different example.

When Barack Hussein Obama was elected and then inaugurated to the office of President of the United States in January 2009 it was fascinating to observe the intensity of adulation. The anticipation as he came to power was immense. The ground-breaking fact of Obama's race appeared to spill over into enormous expectations about his capabilities. At times the atmosphere was almost religious, with Obama being described in messianic terms. (One British newspaper captured the mood with a cartoon image of a fountain in front of the White House bearing a sign: 'Please do not walk on the water'). Why was there such worldwide interest in the forty-fourth president of the United States? Why such a tidal wave of optimism and hope?

As I watched the events unfold, I found myself asking: what are people looking for in a president or, for that matter, in any leader? One of the most insightful answers I came across was written by an American pastor. His piece was titled 'In God we do not trust'. He suggested that the demands that would greet Obama on his first day in the Oval Office indicated the kind of things the world longs for. Two points stood out:

> First, people are longing for a saviour who will atone for their sins. In this election, people are thirsting for a saviour who will atone for their economic sins of buying things they

did not need with money they did not have. The result is a mountain of credit debt they cannot pay and a desperate yearning that somehow a new president will save them from economic hell. Second, people are longing for a king who will keep them safe from terror in his kingdom. In the Old Testament the concept of a peaceable kingdom is marked by the word shalom. In shalom there is not only the absence of sin, war, strife, and suffering but also the presence of love, peace, harmony, and health. And this thirst for shalom is so parched that every election people cannot help but naively believe that, if their candidate simply wins, shalom is sure to come despite sin and the curse.

This assessment rings true. In the acute circumstances of the credit-crunch we long for someone to give us economic stability, but more significantly, we long for an end to evil and terror and for a life of perfect peace and harmony. This is the universal longing of the human heart. Who has the power and the authority to crush evil underfoot and to achieve everlasting peace? The military might of America is certainly great. Perhaps as this is harnessed to the 'smart power' philosophy of Obama's tenure we will see wicked regimes tumble and new life emerging from the ruins. Many hope so. But, whatever his successes, Obama does not have the power to rout the evil in the world with a mere word of rebuke. He does not have the authority to halt the powers of darkness in their tracks simply by speaking. His words cannot guarantee their ultimate demise.

Not even our best leaders can destroy the presence of evil in our world. Fear in the face of terror can stalk every human heart, so what the Bible says about the devil and his work in our world is not so far-fetched. Jesus came to destroy the devil 'and free those who all their lives were held in slavery by their fear of death' (Heb. 2:14). The Bible's view is that the normal fear we feel at the prospect of death is a form of slavery. The world is not meant to be like this. We are not meant to live in fear, but who can stop that happening? Only Jesus, and his absolute authority over evil. The reality of evil in the world is a constant source of fear for us. It was a source of fear for this man in Luke 4 as he found it consumed his life. Jesus turns the tables and makes evil fear him as it stands in his presence, fully aware of who he is. No-one else has the authority to destroy evil like this and demonstrate that their authority is absolute.

Jesus the healer—his tender power

Luke then takes us straight from the synagogue exorcism to a moving bed-side healing. Jesus' healing of Simon's mother-in-law is the first of a string of healing miracles that Luke uses to show us who Jesus is. He can heal, with absolute power over sickness and death, but he does so tenderly. The exorcism brings the 'freedom for the oppressed' that Jesus had mentioned in Luke 4. We therefore learn that knowing Jesus means the absence of fear. Following the exorcism, the healing brings the 'sight for the blind', also mentioned in Luke 4. In this case we learn that knowing Jesus means the presence of his compassion.

One of the scourges of the church is our tendency to avoid one mistake by swinging so seriously in the opposite direction that we end up making another mistake on the other end of the spectrum. There are churches so determined to establish the preaching ministry of Jesus as his priority that they end up portraying him as a callous teacher who has no compassion. Nothing is further from the truth. Notice that Jesus came close to this bed-ridden woman and 'bent over her', breaking the conventions; instead of keeping his distance from the sick and marginalised he comes close. His rebuke is for the disease wracking her body; his powerful care for her as a person is tender. When the day is nearly over and all the sick start flocking to Jesus, he laid his hands 'on each one'. Luke uses this word 'each' to stress the personal nature of Jesus' care for every person that he comes into contact with.

One major point is being established as Luke tells us these facts: the works of Jesus are evidence that the words of Jesus are true. That is to say, if someone stands up in a synagogue and makes extraordinary claims about themselves, and if that same person then casts out demons and walks through a village and heals many sick people, then are we not being given all the evidence we need to believe what he has said? The fact that the works of Jesus go hand in hand with the words of Jesus suggest that this is not a ministry we are to reproduce. In fact much harm is often done by using the miracles of Jesus as a blueprint to bring about healing, rather than as good news to bring about believing. These miracles are not recorded so we can tap into Jesus' power to cure our bodies, but so we can know beyond doubt that Jesus is the one whose teaching and words we can trust. The miracles should help us conclude that Jesus is both Lord and God.

Luke 4:43-44 shows us that Jesus prioritises his preaching ministry over his healing ministry. That is why we should understand the miracles of Jesus as pointers to the truth of his words.

Jesus the preacher—his astonishing priority

This section of Luke begins and ends with Jesus teaching. The focus is Jesus' authoritative word. At the end of the passage Jesus has to remove himself from the crowds who are trying to stop him leaving, precisely because they have not understood what he has come to do. The miracles are so impressive, so appreciated, so wonderful and full of joy. Surely the right thing to do is to get Jesus to stay to see more of them. 'But' he said, surprisingly we may think, 'I must preach the good news of the kingdom of God to the other towns also, because that is why I was sent.' His priority is stated clearly.

If Jesus arrived in our town today and asked us to organise his itinerary what would the priority be? We would have many people clamouring for Jesus to do all sorts of amazing things, but if we recognise what he did as the core of his mission we would organise a preaching tour. If we think there are more important things for Jesus to do, Luke wants to tell us that we're like the people getting in Jesus' way, urgently trying to distract him from his main priority. When exorcisms and miracles are what draw the crowds and grab the headlines, it is astonishing that Jesus wants the spotlight to fall elsewhere: on preaching the good news of the kingdom of God. His dramatic miracles give credence to his powerful words; they are not an end in themselves.

To preach about the 'kingdom of God' was to announce that God had come to reign on earth just as he had promised to do in the Old Testament. The phrase refers to a new world order, one where the demonised, the diseased, and all others living as the outcasts of society would finally be healed, restored, and included in God's family. The kingdom of God means the end of sin and death, and the arrival of perfect peace and happiness. But as Jesus comes and preaches about the kingdom it becomes clear that there is a 'now' and a 'not yet' element to the kingdom. The 'now' element is seen in how Jesus' ministry means a release for captives, it means the end of sickness for those he heals—but it is not universal. That's the 'not yet' aspect. After all, even those he healed eventually died. One day the kingdom of God will extend to the ends of the earth, and what we see Jesus doing in Luke's Gospel we will see happening in the whole world. Death will be defeated. Sickness will be banished. Evil will be destroyed once and for all. This is the good news that Jesus brings.

We need to remember that when Jesus stood up to preach it was God himself speaking. The Old Testament prophets were sent on God's behalf. Sometimes they were listened to, but often they were ignored. Time passed and as history moved on God never lost his loving determination to bring people to know him and be near to him, until at last he appeared himself, in person, to preach. There's nothing like getting the news from the highest authority. People are convinced that they will believe in God if they see a miracle, or if their lottery number comes up, or if all evil comes to an end. Jesus knows that is not true. He knows that people will only believe in God when they hear God speaking to them. This is why preaching is Jesus' priority. Here, in Jesus, God himself addresses the poor and needy people of the world, including you and me. Here, in Jesus' teaching and proclamation, God explains his will and purpose.

Three portraits of Jesus: a deliverer, a healer, and a preacher. But there are also three responses to Jesus in the passage. The demons recognise who Jesus is and bow before his superior power and holiness in silence. Simon's mother-in-law is healed and now serves Jesus in her home. The crowds are utterly amazed at his teachings and his miracles, but they do not see who Jesus is. They try to stop him leaving and are intent on securing his power for themselves and their region only. They do not understand his mission. As we move further into his Gospel, Luke presents us with a sobering fact: it is dangerous to be dazzled and amazed by Jesus' deeds and to be totally oblivious to the priority and meaning of Jesus' words.

4

The Scandal

³⁶ Now one of the Pharisees invited Jesus to have dinner with him, so he went to the Pharisee's house and reclined at the table. ³⁷ When a woman who had lived a sinful life in that town learned that Jesus was eating at the Pharisee's house, she brought an alabaster jar of perfume, ³⁸ and as she stood behind him at his feet weeping, she began to wet his feet with her tears. Then she wiped them with her hair, kissed them and poured perfume on them.

³⁹ When the Pharisee who had invited him saw this, he said to himself, 'If this man were a prophet, he would know who is touching him and what kind of woman she is—that she is a sinner.'

⁴⁰ Jesus answered him, 'Simon, I have something to tell you.'

'Tell me, teacher,' he said.

⁴¹ 'Two men owed money to a certain moneylender. One owed him five hundred denarii, and the other fifty. ⁴² Neither of them had the money to pay him back, so he cancelled the debts of both. Now which of them will love him more?'

[43] Simon replied, 'I suppose the one who had the bigger debt cancelled.'

'You have judged correctly,' Jesus said.

[44] Then he turned toward the woman and said to Simon, 'Do you see this woman? I came into your house. You did not give me any water for my feet, but she wet my feet with her tears and wiped them with her hair. [45] You did not give me a kiss, but this woman, from the time I entered, has not stopped kissing my feet. [46] You did not put oil on my head, but she has poured perfume on my feet. [47] Therefore, I tell you, her many sins have been forgiven—for she loved much. But he who has been forgiven little loves little.'

[48] Then Jesus said to her, 'Your sins are forgiven.'

[49] The other guests began to say among themselves, 'Who is this who even forgives sins?'

[50] Jesus said to the woman, 'Your faith has saved you; go in peace.'

Luke 7:36–50

Finding God

Where would you look to find compelling evidence that God exists?

On 15th January 2009, US Air flight 1549 crashed in the Hudson River in New York. As the plane fell from the sky, the pilot banked to miss George Washington Bridge by nine hundred feet and, in one of the most remarkable feats of skill seen in aviation history, he glided the plane into a perfectly tilted landing on its belly in the water. All one hundred and fifty-five people on board survived the crash. Experts reported that had the positioning of the plane differed even by inches the aircraft would have spun into cartwheels and broken into pieces. After landing, the emergency exits allowed passengers to escape before the cabin flooded and the pilot walked the aisles twice to ensure that everyone was off the plane. Only after he left did the plane begin to sink.

For the rest of that day, and on into the rest of the week, church buildings throughout America were packed with ordinary people so moved by what they had seen that they could not contain their spontaneous thanksgiving to God for the miraculous events on the Hudson. In an unprecedented national response, thousands who otherwise would not describe themselves as religious felt compelled to seek God in a way that they could not fully understand. As queues formed outside churches, irreligious people appeared on television expressing their amazement at God's goodness in what had happened. So spectacular was the deliverance of the lives on the plane, so incredible the precision of the plane's safe landing, that vast numbers of people realised they had seen God's merciful intervention in their world.

If you can remember the news reports from the days following flight 1549's crash landing, you will know that only the first of my previous two paragraphs is true. As some of the passengers from the plane appeared on TV they were some of the most grateful people I have ever seen. The tone of the news reports from witnesses and aviation personnel was one of astonishment. Perhaps some people began to think about God in a new way. But there was none of the national gratitude towards God that I recounted above.

I often meet people who ask questions like: 'How can you believe God exists when terrible things happen in the world?' Sometimes people say, 'I'd believe in God if he ended all the wars; or if he stopped all the suffering in my life.' It is striking that the evidence for God that many people ask for, or even demand from God, is evidence that he never promises or offers. Meanwhile the evidence that he does give us is evidence we often choose to ignore. If all the wars on the globe were to stop tomorrow, would we stop in our tracks and begin praising God? I am sceptical. If anything we would praise our leaders for what they had achieved. When a plane crashes and lives are lost, we pause to wonder where God is and why he didn't do something to stop it. When a plane crashes and not a single life is lost we do not, generally, pause to marvel at the evidence of

God's goodness and grace. Instead, we praise the pilot for his incredible skill (and he should be praised). Yet perhaps God is also giving us the evidence we so often ask for. The evidence for God is all around us if we have eyes to see.

More than this, if we miss the signs of God's presence it may mean we are often looking for God in all the wrong ways. Indeed, in this chapter I want to suggest that the most striking evidence of all is found in some of the most unexpected places. The Bible is not interested in abstract questions about God's existence, and Luke's Gospel is no exception. In this section of Luke, God offers us evidence about himself that is scandalous, embarrassing, distasteful even, if we come to it without a true understanding of ourselves. The truth is that a life changed by God's grace is a more remarkable and profound sign of God's presence than many of the things we claim God should do to convince people of his goodness. This is also an incident where someone who thinks he is rich (Simon) is made to realise that he is miserably poor. A person with a wrong view of themselves is always going to size Jesus up in the wrong way. And someone who knows that they are destitute (the woman) responds to Jesus in a way that is in keeping with who Jesus is, so she finds inestimable treasure. A right view of ourselves enables us to look for God's presence in the right places.

The people Jesus attracts: awkward and indecent

Everything about the woman with her jar of perfume is wrong: who she is, where she is and what she is doing. Luke tells us that this woman 'had lived a sinful life.' This almost certainly identifies her as a prostitute, or at least a woman known for her immorality. But Luke is careful to point out—three times in the space of just two verses—that this encounter takes place in the home of 'a Pharisee'. Simon belonged to a strand of Judaism which was particularly careful to monitor observance of the law and which went to great lengths to distance itself from 'sinners'.

So the scene is set: a prostitute is centre-stage at a gathering of clerics. Instead of doing something to deflect attention, she makes it worse. Bedraggled and broken, weeping in Jesus' presence, she wets his feet with her tears, wipes them with her hair and anoints them with perfume. It was customary for a host to wash his guest's feet with water on arrival. The intensity of the woman's affections, however, made religious leaders squirm in their seats in embarrassment. What will happen?

God is calling this woman from the shadows and the shame of her life to the feet of Jesus Christ, and as he does so the indecent is awkwardly intruding on the religious. That is what happens when God is at work. A woman dismissed by others as immoral, unclean, a social deviant—in short, as 'poor'—is attracted to Jesus while the upright and moral—the 'rich'—look down their noses with pride and disgust.

God's grace is seen in the types of people who are attracted to Jesus. The reality of his grace is profound evidence for God. So while we look around for the evidence of wars stopping, and disasters being avoided, miracles happening and, most important of all, things going well in my life, God says 'No, if you want evidence of my grace—undeniable and sure—would you please look at the type of people who are consistently drawn to my side and into my family.'

Go and visit your local Accident and Emergency department and you will meet the sick and injured in large numbers. They're always there. They go because that's where the doctor is and that's where they will be treated. Similarly, every time you find an authentic gathering of real Christian people, you will find those people who have discovered the grace of Jesus Christ in a world where no one else would give them a second thought. I'm not speaking, of course, about empty religious social clubs that call themselves churches but which are devoid of the presence of Jesus. There are no awkward intrusions there! But among God's people, beside the Lord Jesus, you will see sinners who feel that life has dealt them a rough deal. People like you, people like me; people like us. People who know that we have made a mess of things, and then made a mess of things again. People whose shame is sometimes so great they cannot look another person in the eye. Where God is at work, people like this are always there and it is part of the evidence of the scandalous grace of Jesus Christ. This is the opposite of the popular image of a church full of 'good people'.

But the evidence of grace, as we are about to see, is always an affront to people who think they do not need it.

The knowledge Jesus has: uncomfortable and true

You could have heard a pin drop as everyone wondered what Jesus would do next. Simon the Pharisee is thinking furiously. Someone should usher this vile woman away from his special guest. When he sees that Jesus does nothing to brush her off, silent tut-tuts fill his mind as he forms his thoughts. 'The Messiah? A prophet? No chance. A real prophet would know that he is being touched by the lowest of the low and would have nothing to do with her.'

What happens next is shot through with irony. Simon hasn't spoken at all; we read just his thoughts. Yet in 7:40 we are told that Jesus 'answered' him. In Simon's opinion, Jesus can't be a prophet because of who he's fraternising with. In Luke's opinion, Jesus must be a prophet because he can read Simon's thoughts. Simon shows us that the evidence we want about Jesus is not always the evidence he gives. Simon wants evidence about Jesus that confirms his own view of the world ('I am in the right; this woman is in the wrong'). He wants evidence which means others must be put in their place; evidence of God which will leave him unchanged.

Instead of this, Jesus shows evidence of his power to see into our hearts. Jesus knows exactly how we think. He knows that we are kidding ourselves if we think it's only people who need a crutch to get through life who are attracted to him. Every human being, unless sheer pride prevents them from admitting it, is poverty-stricken and in need of personal deliverance, never mind a crutch. Jesus knows when we look at someone with disdain, when we disapprove of the people he chooses to forgive. He sees the uneasy reluctance in our hearts and the shifty, uncomfortable posture as people we dislike become acquainted with his overwhelming love. Hard, cold, legalistic, ready to blame someone else, we look askance at the lesser mortals of this world and think that they should stay away from someone as important as Jesus. Of course we would never say so! Never. But Jesus knows exactly how we think. Does that make you squirm? It makes me squirm. Jesus can turn the most pleasant dinner party upside down with a word.

It is dangerous to have fixed ideas about people—and especially about Jesus. With compassion and grace, with perfect insight and understanding, he spots the attitudes that are skewed and says 'let me tell you why your thinking has to change'.

The forgiveness Jesus offers: free but offensive

This call to change is precisely what Simon now hears. Jesus tells a story that holds out a mirror for Simon to look in. Although our translation says the parable is about two men, it's literally about two 'debtors'. Two people with bank statements in the red. Even these opening lines are arresting for Simon. He thinks there is only one person in the frame—the woman. No, says Jesus, there are two—you and the woman. You are like a person with a small debt (fifty denarii). She is like a person with a huge debt (five hundred denarii). But then the punch-line of the story slices like a knife: 'Neither of them had the money' to pay back their creditor. Do you get it Simon? Small debt, big debt, no difference: both are bankrupt. Both have nothing. You are on the same playing field. What difference does it make if she has a past as long as her arm? Your life is clean and tidy and you say the right things and do the right things, but the cold and shrivelled nature of your shallow heart means that you are bankrupt too. Do you mean to sit here in my presence and tell me that you are better than her? Simon is moving awkwardly in his seat. Jesus' penetrating teaching exposes the condemnatory self-righteousness that lurks in our hearts. We cannot escape.

The point of Jesus' story, of course, is not to crush Simon or merely expose him. In the parable, 'neither of them had the money to pay him back, so he cancelled the debts of both.' Jesus has come to proclaim good news—the offer of full and free forgiveness. He has come to forgive those who know they are poor and needy like this woman, but who cannot do anything about it themselves. He has come to proclaim forgiveness to those who think they are rich and can see, like Simon, but who are blind to the reality of their bankruptcy.

But this means that if forgiveness is free, it is also offensive. It is offensive to people who cannot see themselves as God sees them. One reason that we, as debtors, fail to see ourselves properly is because we play a trick on ourselves. We play the trick of comparison. My life is not as bad as that person's. The sex offender makes me seem better because I would never do what they did. I can't believe what she has done—it would never enter my head to do that. The problem with all of these things, as I said in the first chapter of this book, is the arbitrary standard we use to make the comparison. What gives me the right to decide the ultimate standard of what is acceptable? That is exactly Simon's mistake. It is a secret attitude of the heart, which Jesus cuts open with all the skill of a master surgeon. 'Your debt may be smaller, Simon, but what good is that if it still leaves you bankrupt? You are in the same boat as this woman.' How much we can make of trivial and false distinctions! Think of passengers in first and second class compartments on an aeroplane, partitioned by a mere curtain, when they are all making the same journey and going to the same destination. So with our standing before God. We separate people into artificial categories of good and bad even though everyone is in need of God's forgiveness. This was Simon the Pharisee's mistake. Luke is showing us that God's forgiveness offends those who think it is only relevant for others.

The love Jesus creates: extravagant and transforming

How different things are for this woman now that she has met Jesus. The story opens with a clear contrast between her as a sinner and Simon as a Pharisee, but it ends with a repeated contrast between their relationships to Jesus. Three times Jesus tells Simon 'You did not...but she...'. Simon did not bathe Jesus' feet, or greet him with a kiss or anoint his head with oil, yet things like this were the basic courtesy of the day. It is not just that the woman has done these things; she has exceeded them. Instead of water and a cloth, she uses her hair and her tears. Instead of one kiss, she has not stopped kissing. Instead of oil, she uses precious perfume.

Jesus does not forgive her because she has done these beautiful things for him. Rather, she loves and adores him in this way because he has forgiven her. Her extravagant love is evidence of extravagant forgiveness. The opposite is also true. Simon's shallow love for Jesus, his most basic hospitality, is evidence of his deep-seated conviction that he does not need Jesus because he thinks he has little or no need of forgiveness.

If someone forgives you this week for bashing into their heels with your supermarket trolley, you will soon forget about the forgiveness you have received. If it happens, you will quickly say 'Oh I'm very sorry, so sorry.' The injured shopper usually says to you (as they limp along for a few seconds), 'Don't worry, it doesn't matter. I'm fine.' Normally, unless there is an unusual case of trolley-rage, nothing else will be thought about it. A small wrong was committed, and that small misdeed has been forgiven. You will not feel compelled to stay in touch with the person, or to write them a long letter of undying gratitude for their kindness in forgiving you so readily.

But how should we respond if we have been forgiven for some terrible misdemeanour? I can assure you that you would blush were I to list all the sins that Jesus has forgiven me. What if we were to list each of our sins in a diary? All the bitterness and lies, the attitudes and addictions and lusts, the harsh words and selfish greed, the pampered existence in the face of a starving world. Our diaries would be multi-volume works! For all of us, the awful scale of every ugly sin, every bit of rebellion against God, every last spot and stain is so vast. If Jesus can forgive it all, wipe the slate clean, and embrace you and me with all our indecency and shame, how should we respond to him?

If Jesus were to visit my church on any Sunday, two groups of people would soon emerge. There would be the polite, circumspect, but cool and formal group. They would think about protocol and quickly organise a system whereby the most 'important' would get to meet Jesus in an orderly and arranged manner. Then there would be the other group—a source of scandalous embarrassment in their desire to push to the front, to touch him, embrace him, and weep before him. Those most conscious of sins and failings, and most grateful for forgiveness and mercy: natural, lavish, extravagant in their love. Which group would you join?

We shouldn't assume that loving Christ lavishly will mean that all who do so are naturally expressive or extravagant people. From the quiet shadows of sin-crushed lives and the hidden corners of burdened shame, all sorts of people would come. People who know that Jesus has forgiven them cannot help but love him deeply. If we have been forgiven so much and so freely, the evidence will be there in our depth of love, however we show it. We get glimpses of this all the time: when people sing, or pray, or cry, or stay in touch with someone long after everyone else has forgotten. We notice the person who gives and gives and gives, and then gives some more. We see it in the person who waits, and prays, and shares, and makes sacrifices for Christ's people, because they love Christ more than anyone or anything else in all the world.

We don't ultimately know how Simon responded to Jesus, but we do know that the woman left in peace. Can you imagine how she felt after leaving the Pharisee's house? She had a dignity and a serenity that she had never known. She arrived as a damaged scrap of humanity from the gutter of society, and she left as a restored and renewed woman. Every other man had used, degraded, and then discarded her. But not Jesus.

Have you seen the scandal in Luke 7:36–50? It is there in abundance. There is the scandal of Simon looking for the wrong evidence in all the wrong places. He is looking for evidence 'out there'; busy looking at someone else's sin instead of his own need. There is the scandal of a life of shame and sin being wiped clean and forgiven. There is the scandal of the hard-heart in the presence of such love and compassion. There is the scandal of the ability to look askance at others while being blind to the reality about ourselves.

Luke intends us to see ourselves in the story: we're either like Simon, or we're like this woman. You will know as you read these lines which of them your life mirrors most closely. Tidy, organised, religious, respectable; or broken, ashamed, regretful, restless. When we see ourselves in Simon, or when we see ourselves in this woman, then we are not really helped by evidence of some distant, remote, higher power ordering events in our world. What we need is a Saviour. Grace, undeserved forgiveness, is the evidence we need. When we see grace like this we meet someone who can challenge us to the core of our beings and whose mercy can flood our lives to transform us forever. 'Come near to me,' Jesus says. 'Come in faith like this woman did and know that I am able to forgive you for everything.'

5

The Greatest Mistakes
You Could Ever Make

¹³ Someone in the crowd said to him, 'Teacher, tell my brother to divide the inheritance with me.'

¹⁴ Jesus replied, 'Man, who appointed me a judge or an arbiter between you?' ¹⁵Then he said to them, 'Watch out! Be on your guard against all kinds of greed; a man's life does not consist in the abundance of his possessions.'

¹⁶And he told them this parable: 'The ground of a certain rich man produced a good crop. ¹⁷He thought to himself, "What shall I do? I have no place to store my crops."

¹⁸ 'Then he said, "This is what I'll do. I will tear down my barns and build bigger ones, and there I will store all my grain and my goods. ¹⁹And I'll say to myself, 'You have plenty of good things laid up for many years. Take life easy; eat, drink and be merry.'"

²⁰ 'But God said to him, "You fool! This very night your life will be demanded from you. Then who will get what you have prepared for yourself?"

²¹ 'This is how it will be with anyone who stores up things for himself but is not rich toward God.'

²² Then Jesus said to his disciples: 'Therefore I tell you, do not worry about your life, what you will eat; or about your body, what you will wear. ²³ Life is more than food, and the body more than clothes. ²⁴ Consider the ravens: They do not sow or reap, they have no storeroom or barn; yet God feeds them. And how much more valuable you are than birds! ²⁵ Who of you by worrying can add a single hour to his life? ²⁶ Since you cannot do this very little thing, why do you worry about the rest?

²⁷ 'Consider how the lilies grow. They do not labour or spin. Yet I tell you, not even Solomon in all his splendour was dressed like one of these. ²⁸ If that is how God clothes the grass of the field, which is here today, and tomorrow is thrown into the fire, how much more will he clothe you, O you of little faith! ²⁹ And do not set your heart on what you will eat or drink; do not worry about it. ³⁰ For the pagan world runs after all such things, and your Father knows that you need them. ³¹ But seek his kingdom, and these things will be given to you as well.

³² 'Do not be afraid, little flock, for your Father has been pleased to give you the kingdom. ³³ Sell your possessions and give to the poor. Provide purses for yourselves that will not wear out, a treasure in heaven that will not be exhausted, where no thief comes near and no moth destroys. ³⁴ For where your treasure is, there your heart will be also.

³⁵ 'Be dressed ready for service and keep your lamps burning, ³⁶ like men waiting for their master to return from a wedding banquet, so that when he comes and knocks they can immediately open the door for him. ³⁷ It will be good for those servants whose master finds them watching when he comes. I tell you the truth, he will dress himself to serve, will have them recline at the table and will come and wait on them. ³⁸ It will be good for those servants whose master finds them ready, even if he comes in the second or third watch of the night. ³⁹ But understand this: If the owner of the house had known at what hour the thief was coming, he would not have let his house be broken into. ⁴⁰ You also must be ready, because

the Son of Man will come at an hour when you do not expect him.'

[41] Peter asked, 'Lord, are you telling this parable to us, or to everyone?'

[42] The Lord answered, 'Who then is the faithful and wise manager, whom the master puts in charge of his servants to give them their food allowance at the proper time? [43] It will be good for that servant whom the master finds doing so when he returns. [44] I tell you the truth, he will put him in charge of all his possessions. [45] But suppose the servant says to himself, "My master is taking a long time in coming," and he then begins to beat the menservants and maidservants and to eat and drink and get drunk. [46] The master of that servant will come on a day when he does not expect him and at an hour he is not aware of. He will cut him to pieces and assign him a place with the unbelievers.

[47] 'That servant who knows his master's will and does not get ready or does not do what his master wants will be beaten with many blows. [48] But the one who does not know and does things deserving punishment will be beaten with few blows. From everyone who has been given much, much will be demanded; and from the one who has been entrusted with much, much more will be asked.'

Luke 12:13–48

Getting it wrong

It was just a simple, honest mistake.

A couple of years ago, a friend of mine offered to book plane tickets for his parents-in-law for their visit to Aberdeen. He went online and booked them return flights from Heathrow to Aberdeen. Or so he thought. Two days before they were due to fly, his mother-in-law phoned to say that she had just looked at the tickets, and the flights were booked in the wrong direction. Although they were living in London, the tickets were from Aberdeen to London and back again! They had to get the train.

Luke 12 is all about making mistakes. Jesus' words in this

chapter have an automatic connection to our lives because we all know what it means to get something wrong. A word out of place, a lapse of concentration, a little oversight and suddenly we're landed with a mistake that leaves us cringing in shame and embarrassment. The email sent to the whole office when you only meant to send it to one person, the car keys locked in the boot, the birthday or anniversary completely forgotten. Of course, other mistakes have far more serious consequences: the marriage torn apart by a one-night stand, the resignation offered in anger, the safety precaution at work ignored in haste. The mistakes Jesus talks about are even more serious than any of these. Make one of these mistakes, we're told, and we don't just lose face but are in danger of losing everything. Jesus is clear and the lines of challenge to us are drawn directly.

He speaks so starkly in this chapter because of who he's talking to. The opening verse says 'Meanwhile, when a crowd of many thousands had gathered, so that they were trampling on one another, Jesus began to speak first to his disciples' (12:1). Jesus' popularity is sky-high. He's the latest, greatest thing and everyone wants in on the action. But Jesus isn't interested in admirers, however sincere in their admiration; he wants devoted followers. So as Jesus turns to his disciples and speaks to them he's engaging in a sifting process, setting down challenges which will expose the true disciple from the curious onlooker. 'Everyone seems to want me,' Jesus is saying, 'well, do they? Let me tell you about all the common mistakes my true followers need to avoid.' Don't make the mistake of thinking that God does not see and hear everything you do and say (12:2). What a terrible error to be afraid of the terrorist who can kill but to not give a second thought to standing before Almighty God on judgment day (12:4). Are you considering turning your back on me? To do so would be a catastrophic mistake because it will lead to me turning my back on you (12:9).

The three mistakes in Luke 12:13–48, which we will look at in this chapter, are: thinking about my wealth as if God is not there, worrying about my needs as if God does not care, and focusing on the present as if Jesus is not returning.

Thinking about my wealth as if God is not there

In Luke 12:13, someone in the crowd asks Jesus to do something that we might think is reasonable. 'Teacher, tell my brother to divide the inheritance with me.' They say that where there's a will, there's a war. But this request seems fair enough; after all, fifty-fifty is an equal share. But Jesus' answer is striking: 'Watch out, be on your guard against all kinds of greed' (12:15). He responds in a way that punctures pretence and cuts to the heart of the issue. For the crowd, for the thousands flocking to him, it's normal to think 'I'll have Jesus, but I'll have my riches too. They look lovely together; a little bit of religion, a lot of wealth.' But what the world says is normal, Jesus says could be a disastrous form of greed, a sign of misplaced priorities. Isn't that stark? We make wills and it is normal to receive an inheritance. Yet Jesus says that genuine disciples in his kingdom will see an inheritance as a possible danger. The danger is not the inheritance, the danger is not riches or wealth. The danger is thinking about them as if God is not there. So Jesus tells a parable about a 'certain rich man' (12:16).

It is easy to imagine the scenario. The rich man has worked hard all his life. Shrewd investments mean his pension hasn't gone down the drain and his stocks and shares have come good at the right time. As he surveys all that he has, he decides to expand his portfolio and buy a country estate. He plans a party. He prepares to invite all his friends from the golf club, and he orders the best food and wine. Then, as he stands on his balcony overlooking his land, he has a heart attack and is dead before his wine glass hits the floor.

His is the leading obituary in the papers. He was so well connected, so well known; his wise investments had won him many friends and admirers down through the years. Naturally, the obituary hails him as a success. Look at everything he had achieved and everything he owned. He was unlucky, yes, because just as he was about to relax and enjoy everything he had worked for, he died. 'Unlucky, but definitely a success.' That's what the papers would say, that would be the sound-bite on the news. That's what the crowds would say as they press Jesus for some helpful advice about how to get along in the world.

Look what God says in his obituary: 'You Fool' (12:20). In the Bible, a fool is not someone who is a bit dim or hasn't been educated—it's someone who says there's no God. That means the world is full of professorial and professional fools. Degree certificates line their study walls, but with their lives they proudly reject God. They live as if this life is all there is. They live as if God is not there. God says people like this are fools.

We don't know much about the man in the parable. We don't know whether he was a good man or a bad man, whether he mistreated his employees or was kind. But we know he was self-absorbed. He speaks constantly about himself. His only concern is what he will do, what he will build, what he will store. It's me, me, me all the way. What he learns in a painfully abrupt way is that God sees these hidden attitudes of the heart: 'you prepared all this for yourself.'

When the wealthy person dies, what we always want to know is how much did they leave? The answer Jesus gives is that they leave everything. The real question is: who did they leave it to? If their wealth is only for themselves then it's a waste; if their wealth is given to God then that's an investment that will last forever. That's what verse 21 means: it doesn't mean that anyone who is selfishly rich will always drop dead! It means that when God calls time, anyone who is selfishly rich will find that they've poured their life into negative equity.

As I log on to online banking, my bank is not interested in reminding me about God. He's not listed as an account option. There's no pop-up advert gently encouraging me to be generous. Rather, what I see are adverts about new mortgage contracts, a new insurance policy, the option of a new loan, sign after sign telling me that my security comes from putting my money in the right place. Instead, Jesus says to the serious disciple: 'Watch out! Be warned! The day will come when you will die and it may come sooner than you think. If you have invested primarily in yourself and your concerns then you have made a terrible mistake—for your investment will die with you.'

Worrying about my needs as if God does not care

As I hear the ringing clarity of Jesus' words they are both incredibly attractive and deeply unsettling. I don't want to be all ears for Jesus for a short while but then drop out when I see what it costs. I want to be a disciple. But this vision of a life lived for God—with everything I own given to him and not used for me only—is also unsettling. If I'm so rich towards God that I'm only just making ends meet, what about my family? Will we survive? How will we get by? Jesus anticipates exactly that reaction. So he teaches us how to avoid another mistake. 'Therefore, I tell you, do not worry about your life, what you will eat; or about your body, what you will wear' (12:22).

The logic here in these verses is that of proportional value. God cares for ravens, which have no bank accounts or storehouses; God takes time to dress the flowers of the field magnificently, yet their life span is incredibly short. So if God does that for birds and grass, when seen in proportion, do you really think he's going to forget about you? You are much more valuable so don't think that God does not care about your needs.

Whereas the rich man's mistake was that of pride in his own achievements, the disciple's mistake is often to worry about their own needs. Of course, for many of us in the western world, our comfort is such that we never need to worry about what to wear, we don't worry about where the next set of clothes is coming from; we're more likely to worry about what not to eat or wear! But even with all our wealth, many marriages would reveal that finances are one of the biggest causes of arguments, even with competitors like our health, children, or relatives.

Jesus says that lots of worry comes from having little faith (12:28). The things I worry about are the things I think God cannot cope with and my worry is, at root, a way of saying to God, 'you do not care'. By connecting worry to lack of faith, Jesus shows that worry is always a sign of misplaced trust: trust in me, trust in my money, trust in what I have, trust in what I can provide, trust in what I can fix. Jesus asks, 'Why do you trust the untrustworthy? Why trust your wealth when it can disappear tomorrow?' (12:33). The point of Jesus' words is to encourage those who want to follow him to lift their horizons beyond this world to the next world and to the prospect of heaven. That is the only location for a sound investment. 'Provide purses for yourselves that will not wear out, a treasure in heaven that will not be exhausted, where no thief comes near and no moth destroys. For,' Jesus states with disturbing clarity, 'where your treasure is, there your heart will be also' (12:33-4).

Jesus is not speaking about your physical heart pumping blood around your body. By referring to the 'heart', Jesus means a person's spiritual will, the driving force of the personality. Our heart will belong to whatever we treasure. Jesus sees through our human tendency to think we can split ourselves in many different directions at once in a way that is truly satisfying. While some are better at multi-tasking than others, Jesus teaches that no-one can multi-worship. We are designed by God to worship in only one direction. To worship is to give my entire life, my allegiance, my honour and service to someone or something. We each have only one heart of love and one treasure to cherish. Every person either longs for this world or the next, either worships Jesus or not, either worships the true God or not. Jesus is not expecting his disciples to be able to treasure him in an instant. Rather, he is talking about the governing attitude of my life. Is my focus, my priority, my passion, Christ and his kingdom or something else?

The disciples desperately needed to understand that. They were surrounded constantly by crowds who wanted a little bit of Jesus and a little bit of everything else. Anyone who wants to follow Jesus today needs to understand this. It is the difference between admiring Jesus from a distance, a religious ornament on the immaculate shelf of a tidy and self-centred life; or adoring Jesus up close in his presence as you realise that there is nothing and no-one more precious. This is the discovery that the disciples made, and which we must make all over again, or for the first time if we have never made it before. To know and worship the Lord Jesus Christ is not a little better than other life choices. It is in a different order altogether. This Saviour's love is treasure that makes everything else, even so many of God's good gifts to us, seem like dust and debris by comparison.

Jesus is not calling his disciples to take leave of their senses and go against their instincts and powers of reason. Rather he is telling them to act on the evidence of what they have seen of his glorious kingdom. It is the same for us. Read, observe, listen to Jesus, watch him with the outcasts. Listen to his unfolding and cataclysmic descriptions of what is going to happen to this world, take heed of your life, think about your sin and God's anger, and then look at the mercy of the Lord Jesus. Chew it over, watch, take it in, pray. If after doing that you are able to examine Jesus and conclude that there is nothing of worth, then my response is to say 'Well, turn your back, live life and be merry.' Either respond like that, or worship him with everything you have—heart, soul, mind, strength, possessions, career, family—but nothing in between. Please, nothing in between.

Focusing on the present as if Jesus is not returning

The two mistakes that we have looked at closely in Luke 12 are really only one mistake: thinking that the present is more important than the future.

When Jesus says that the future matters more than the present we should realise that nothing is more likely to make the crowds slowly dwindle away. Is it any wonder Jesus had a small band of disciples and not a stadium packed with admirers at the end of his ministry? Who wants to invest in something we can't see, a kingdom we can't touch? 'We didn't come to hear you for this, Jesus; we're not interested in this.' Christ's teaching about these mistakes comes to a head with one final great warning: do not forget that Jesus is coming back.

This is the point of the story that begins in verse 35. Jesus being absent from our world is like a master being away on business. His servants are meant to be waiting for him to return, ready to receive him at any moment. You can imagine the rumours beginning to circulate. 'He's been gone awfully long hasn't he? Did he actually say he'd be back or did we make it up?' Only the servant who believes that what the master says is true and who believes that he's coming back will be ready when he does so. The true follower of Jesus lives in the present in a way which is ready for his return at any hour. You can see from the end of the passage just how serious this is.

The imagery in these verses is that of company employment and financial investment. While the CEO is out of the office, the employees have several investment choices to make. The big mistake on view here is the issue of wrong investment. It is, surely, folly to invest in my personal kingdom instead of Christ's kingdom. For the faithful servant, the motivation for this investment is not fear but a stunning reward: 'It will be good for those servants whose master finds them watching when he comes. I tell you the truth, he will dress himself to serve, will have them recline at the table and will come and wait on them' (12:37). Isn't that the one thing that would never happen? Normally, the master comes home and as the servant opens the door he may not even say 'thank you.' Servants are not there to be spoken to, but should be like oil in the machinery of life, hidden but helpful.

But this is the Jesus I know and love. He was a servant in his lifetime on earth among us, and he will be a servant at the end of time as he comes for those who have lived and longed for his return. It is the depth of Jesus' love for us that compels his true followers to be watchful. It is the kind of master he is and the way in which he treats his servants that draws our constant gaze. There is no one we would rather see, no one we would rather wait for.

If we understand the dangers lurking in wealth, worry and the future, and we see what Jesus is warning us against, the picture he paints of life in his kingdom is wonderful. Jesus gives us a serious warning: be rich towards God. He shows us a gracious Father: he will provide. And he makes clear promises: one day he will return to serve those who love him and to judge those who turn their backs on him.

When you meet someone who has grasped the riches of a life like this in Christ's kingdom you will find something unusual. You will see a person who is never as wealthy in this life as they could be, while the people they rub shoulders with always become richer than they might otherwise be. The person who embraces Jesus loosens their grip on everything else. They give their money to others. They share their home with strangers. They are not obsessed with their own nearest and dearest. They spend time with the unlovely. They shift their priorities from themselves to others. Their worries about the present shrink while their hopes for the future grow. Their perspective is dominated by what is coming soon, not what is happening now. All because Jesus Christ is the greatest treasure they possess.

6

The Back to Front Kingdom

¹ One Sabbath, when Jesus went to eat in the house of a prominent Pharisee, he was being carefully watched. ² There in front of him was a man suffering from dropsy. ³ Jesus asked the Pharisees and experts in the law, 'Is it lawful to heal on the Sabbath or not?' ⁴ But they remained silent. So taking hold of the man, he healed him and sent him away.

⁵ Then he asked them, 'If one of you has a son or an ox that falls into a well on the Sabbath day, will you not immediately pull him out?' ⁶ And they had nothing to say.

⁷ When he noticed how the guests picked the places of honour at the table, he told them this parable: ⁸ 'When someone invites you to a wedding feast, do not take the place of honour, for a person more distinguished than you may have been invited. ⁹ If so, the host who invited both of you will come and say to you, 'Give this man your seat.' Then, humiliated, you will have to take the least important place. ¹⁰ But when you are invited, take the lowest place, so that when your host comes, he will say to you, 'Friend, move up to a better place.' Then you will be honoured

in the presence of all your fellow guests. [11] For everyone who exalts himself will be humbled, and he who humbles himself will be exalted.'

[12] Then Jesus said to his host, 'When you give a luncheon or dinner, do not invite your friends, your brothers or relatives, or your rich neighbours; if you do, they may invite you back and so you will be repaid. [13] But when you give a banquet, invite the poor, the crippled, the lame, the blind, [14] and you will be blessed. Although they cannot repay you, you will be repaid at the resurrection of the righteous.'

[15] When one of those at the table with him heard this, he said to Jesus, 'Blessed is the man who will eat at the feast in the kingdom of God.'

[16] Jesus replied: 'A certain man was preparing a great banquet and invited many guests. [17] At the time of the banquet he sent his servant to tell those who had been invited, "Come, for everything is now ready."

[18] 'But they all alike began to make excuses. The first said, "I have just bought a field, and I must go and see it. Please excuse me."

[19] 'Another said, "I have just bought five yoke of oxen, and I'm on my way to try them out. Please excuse me."

[20] 'Still another said, "I just got married, so I can't come."

[21] 'The servant came back and reported this to his master. Then the owner of the house became angry and ordered his servant, "Go out quickly into the streets and alleys of the town and bring in the poor, the crippled, the blind and the lame."

[22] '"Sir," the servant said, "what you ordered has been done, but there is still room."

[23] 'Then the master told his servant, "Go out to the roads and country lanes and make them come in, so that my house will be full. [24] I tell you, not one of those men who were invited will get a taste of my banquet."'

Luke 14:1–24

Watching me, watching you

Never could you imagine someone more in command than Jesus at this dinner party. The incident takes place at the house of a prominent Pharisee. This in itself is enough to make us realise that Jesus is not among friends. If you were to find yourself in a situation where all eyes are on you, where you know you are under scrutiny, where you are sure the people watching you have no integrity and little love for you, what would you do?

Luke leaves us in no doubt about who is in control. We're told that Jesus was being 'carefully watched'. Yet twice he addresses the Pharisees directly and leaves them with nothing at all to say. As if this was not enough, Luke tells us (v. 7) that while they are watching Jesus, he has been watching them. What he observes is more than a failure of manners. It is a failure of character and morality, of love for God and others, and Jesus is about to expose it in the most penetrating way imaginable. The one whose public actions are under scrutiny is the one who is scrutinising the secrets of the heart.

We might expect that a world of cultured, intellectual and religious dignitaries is the least likely setting for a robust challenge. But Jesus is strong enough and loving enough to break every known social convention to get through to the people gathered in that home. An evening of polite conversation that sounds sincere, but which skilfully avoids any topic or issue that could cause awkwardness or offence, can be an agonising experience. Many of us, I suspect, dragged along by a well intentioned spouse, would enter the Pharisee's home longing to be anywhere else. But anyone thinking that the dinner party at the Pharisee's house would be dull was in for a massive shock. Jesus is never dull, he is not always comforting, but he is always truthful—no less so when talking to religious people.

It is a mark of the extraordinary depth of Jesus' love that he was willing to reach out a hand of divine grace, not only to the sick man whom he healed, but also to the proud self-sufficient dinner guests who looked on with disapproval. In reaching out in this way, Jesus turned a world of religious pomposity on its head and shows us that when it comes to entering God's kingdom everything is back to front. True religion is not what we think it is. God is not who we so often think he is. Those we assume Jesus would pass by turn out to be the ones he welcomes. Those who think their front row seats in the kingdom are secure and guaranteed turn up to find the door locked. And in a further incident from Luke 18 we will see that the person who has nothing to offer God but their sin is the person who finds that God offers them everything.

The back to front priorities of sanctimonious religion

In Luke 13, Jesus presents us with stark warnings about people being locked out of God's kingdom. These are warnings Jesus wants the world to hear. But how will the world respond? What will people do when they hear the gospel? How will complacent, religious, hardened, cynical people respond to such challenges? Luke gives us the answer in chapter 14.

Much of the baggage we carry around with us is like an inoculation against catching a real dose of love for Jesus Christ. Out of love for these sanctimonious and complacent people—so full of humbug and hot-air—Jesus brings them back to basics. It's as if Jesus sweeps his arm across the table, clearing onto the floor all the finery and pretence that people often expect Almighty God to notice. In itself this is astonishing, for when most of us come up against empty religious waffle we either avoid it like the plague, or go along with it by default. But not Jesus—his love is more radical than that. He is too radical to avoid such people, too real to copy them, so he speaks into their midst in a confrontational and potentially explosive manner.

What does Jesus say? He doesn't say anything directly to the cynical Pharisees. First, he lets them watch as he does the unmentionable and heals a man on the Sabbath. They hate the fact that Jesus has healed this man. How could he! How could he do that! It is appalling, a desecration, a slap in the face for his host and an insult to their cherished traditions. Perhaps we don't often think of Jesus causing such major offence. Yet he does. Then, with offended ears and eyes all waiting for his defence, then and only then he speaks to them and brings the brilliant light of his love into the stifling darkness of their hideously arid religious gathering.

With one simple question he reduces them to silence. Would you lift your son out of a well on the Sabbath if he fell into it? Would you? Come on, answer the question! They have nothing to say. Jesus has impaled them on the cold logic of their bitter disapproval. Their religious priorities are the reverse of what they should be. They would look after their own child, certainly, for that is the extent of their love. But they would not contemplate loving another person by rejoicing in their healing. One thing at home; another thing in public to be seen to be keeping the letter of the law. Do you know people like that? Are you like that?

But the searchlight of Jesus' loving scrutiny is just beginning to probe the darkness of their hearts. Having watched them all jostling for pride of place at the table, with their embarrassment and discomfort becoming more and more palpable, Jesus goes on to explain that recognition and applause eludes those who want them. Recognition is like a slippery bar of soap, and if you spend your life seeking the honour and approval of others then that is the one thing that will slip from your grasp. You will end up a twisted, bitter old has-been with not a scrap of anything to show for your life's consuming passion. To seek to be first now is a sure-fire way to end up being last. But if you live in a back to front way and count yourself as nothing now, then in God's kingdom you will find true recognition.

Now that he has embarrassed the guests, Jesus turns to address the host himself. You can feel the tension. 'Now,

Mr Host, Mr Prominent Pharisee in your robes and finery, let me tell you a thing or two about throwing a party.'

The back to front invitation of an extravagant host

'Don't be so dull, so predictable and boring as to invite your friends and family. If you do that then it's abundantly clear that the only thing you are doing is trying to get an invite in return. No, when you invite people for a meal, be like God and invite the people who smell, and whose house you would never want to enter, let alone eat anything in. Make your invitation cards out to the people who have never been to a dinner party in their lives. Then you will get a different kind of reward.'

Latching on to Jesus' words, and obviously trying to calm things down a bit, someone at the table pipes up in verse 15: 'Blessed is the man who will eat at the feast in the kingdom of God.' He may as well have exclaimed 'Well said! Now how is the weather doing outside?' It is just pretentious waffle to try and evade what Jesus is talking about, and Jesus will not tolerate it. This is the kind of baggage that he is so determined to sweep right off the table. But a shouting match wouldn't work. Nor would a mere debate. Rather, Jesus tells a parable, and he does so with insight and power.

The back to front excuses of the eventually excluded

This is a story about a man preparing a great banquet. The invitations are sent out. Then, as was the custom, the second invitation is sent out when the moment arrives for the banquet to begin. The guests give the most lame and feeble excuses imaginable.

'I've bought a field—and I need to go and see it.'

What a load of rubbish. You never bought a field without looking at it first.

'I've just bought five yoke of oxen, and I'm on my way to try them out. Please excuse me.'

It's a slap in the face to the man who prepared the banquet.

'I just got married, so I can't come.'

These people, who didn't even have the decency to say that they'd rather not come at the time of the first invitation, are insolent and disgracefully rude.

Luke wants us to take in the fact that God is preparing a banquet. The banquet will be served in the future. Just like the extravagant host who sent his servant to announce the banquet, God sent Jesus his Son into the world to issue the invitation. But Jesus is faced with all the lame excuses as religious people consistently show by their feeble response that they would prefer almost anything to his kingdom. Any excuse will do to get him off my back; whatever I can think of to make Jesus go away.

I have discovered that often it is the same people who make excuses when they hear of Christ's invitation who get upset when they hear that God is angry at our sin and our rebellion. Certainly it is not fashionable to believe in a God who is angry or is going to judge the world. But Jesus says that our baggage and excuses, our dilly-dallying and delays, our insolence and our complacency when faced with an invitation to his kingdom, all of these will eventually disqualify us from entry.

We don't know who spoke next at the dinner table. Did someone clear their throat and ask for the salt to be passed? Luke doesn't tell us. That is because he wants us to read the parable and to be every bit as stunned and shocked as those proud dinner guests were that day. He wants us to ask: 'Can this be right, Lord, that you would show such lavish love as this? Isn't this gospel business going just a bit too far? Lord, are you really saying that people who are not fit for life in your kingdom end up at your table? Dragged in off the streets, just because some others refused your invitation? Lord, should your kingdom really fill up in that way? Isn't there some kind of limit to this extraordinary grace—whereby complete no-hopers can walk in just because they happened to be in the right place at the right time?'

Jesus says 'Yes, that's exactly what I'm saying. These people are friends at my table and guests at a party they had never even dreamt of attending.' This is an astonishing reality. Some people, those who have flung the invitation of the Lord Jesus back in his face, will complain to the bitter end that they are excluded when they could have been there! But the grace of God always leaves some people getting harder and harder, and angrier and angrier. I have met people like this—so knotted up about Jesus that they would do anything they could to kill him. I know others too who love Jesus more and more as they see that they should have been left outside, but now find themselves invited to the banquet.

Now you might be asking: what does it look like in reality to be the religiously proud person that God excludes from his kingdom, and what does it look like to be the unsuspecting outcast who ends up at his table? So before we finish this chapter there are two other people I want you to meet. They show us the back to front kingdom. To meet them, we need to move from the party to the temple. After all, isn't that where we would expect to find religious people doing what they do best?

[9] To some who were confident of their own righteousness and looked down on everybody else, Jesus told this parable: [10] 'Two men went up to the temple to pray, one a Pharisee and the other a tax collector. [11] The Pharisee stood up and prayed about himself: "God, I thank you that I am not like other men—robbers, evildoers, adulterers—or even like this tax collector. [12] I fast twice a week and give a tenth of all I get."

[13] 'But the tax collector stood at a distance. He would not even look up to heaven, but beat his breast and said, "God, have mercy on me, a sinner."

[14] 'I tell you that this man, rather than the other, went home justified before God. For everyone who exalts himself will be humbled, and he who humbles himself will be exalted.'

Luke 18:9–14

The back to front forgiveness of a merciful Saviour

We lose the impact of this parable when we read the words 'Pharisee' and 'tax-collector'. If we insert the words 'minister' and 'paedophile' we are approaching the shocking and revolutionary heart of what Jesus is saying.

Imagine these two men. The first so at home in the church. So confident of his own abilities and qualities. So ready to see the sins, faults, failings and mistakes of everyone else. He is the person whom the whole world would imagine is up at the top of the tree in the kingdom of God. The other man is a public disgrace. Hated and reviled by the whole community. He is an outcast, not just because of his actual sins, but because of the stigma that he can never get away from and his collusion with other people who are also resented. But the greatest difference between the two (and ultimately it is the only significant difference between the two), is that one has caught a glimpse of God's mercy whereas the other has never seen beyond his religious pedigree and his profound self-confidence.

The despised outcast humbles himself, is forgiven and goes home a new man; the ardent religious devotee exalts himself, thinks he has no need of forgiveness and goes home as proud and lost as when he arrived.

If you are reading this book as someone who feels ashamed or shabby about your past, even the recent past; if you are full of thoughts about those whom you have let down, and those you have cheated in some way; if crowding into your mind and obliterating your view of Jesus are all the reasons Jesus probably wouldn't want much to do with you, then it is clear from this parable that what Jesus wants to do is to come over to you, in your secret corner of shame and sorrow. He wants to lift up your head and say 'I know everything about you. Even though I do, if in your heart you are crying for forgiveness, then you will be justified—declared not guilty, the slate wiped clean and given a fresh start with me.'

It is worth pausing here to realise just how back to front this is. Everything in our world wants to reject and recoil from such a notion of undeserved and unmerited favour. Recently I gave a beggar a sandwich outside Waverly Station in Edinburgh. As I gave it to him, I was struck by the fact that he would not lift his face and look at me. That is what rejection, or despair, or fear, or crushing guilt can do to a person. It is exactly what the man in Jesus' parable was experiencing (v. 13).

But here Jesus tells us that the living God has a way of reaching into his fallen and broken world and taking hold of the outcast and the rebel, while by-passing the proud and the morally upright. He by-passes the healthy who imagine they have no need for his gospel medicine. Instead, he stoops beside those who, in the midst of shame and rejection, say 'Lord have mercy on me.' And he does what I could not do for the beggar outside the station. He lifts up the head of the humble sinner, and he says 'you are a forgiven child in my family, and one day you will be exalted to a place at my banquet. One day you will be seated beside others who, despite their track record, have received the gift of eternal life.'

If having read these parables you are still unsure whether you are more a religious Pharisee than a humble sinner, then you would be the same as many church-going and upstanding members of our communities. Each one of us, whatever our successes in life, whatever our track record of decency, religion and honest hard work, has to come to the point of saying to Jesus, 'Lord, I need your mercy'. It takes something as shocking as Jesus' parables to help us to see this. It takes nothing less than the mercy of Jesus to bring us into his family. The last minute guests at the dinner party, the sinner in the temple, and we too—if we experience it—can never forget and never ask for anything more valuable than the mercy of Jesus Christ.

7

Finders Keepers

[1] Now the tax collectors and 'sinners' were all gathering around to hear him. [2] But the Pharisees and the teachers of the law muttered, 'This man welcomes sinners and eats with them.'

[3] Then Jesus told them this parable: [4] 'Suppose one of you has a hundred sheep and loses one of them. Does he not leave the ninety-nine in the open country and go after the lost sheep until he finds it? [5] And when he finds it, he joyfully puts it on his shoulders [6] and goes home. Then he calls his friends and neighbours together and says, "Rejoice with me; I have found my lost sheep." [7] I tell you that in the same way there will be more rejoicing in heaven over one sinner who repents than over ninety-nine righteous persons who do not need to repent.

[8] 'Or suppose a woman has ten silver coins and loses one. Does she not light a lamp, sweep the house and search carefully until she finds it? [9] And when she finds it, she calls her friends and neighbours together and says, "Rejoice with me; I have found my lost coin." [10] In the same way, I tell you, there is rejoicing in the presence of the angels of God over one sinner who repents.'

¹¹ Jesus continued: 'There was a man who had two sons. ¹² The younger one said to his father, "Father, give me my share of the estate." So he divided his property between them.

¹³ 'Not long after that, the younger son got together all he had, set off for a distant country and there squandered his wealth in wild living. ¹⁴ After he had spent everything, there was a severe famine in that whole country, and he began to be in need. ¹⁵ So he went and hired himself out to a citizen of that country, who sent him to his fields to feed pigs. ¹⁶ He longed to fill his stomach with the pods that the pigs were eating, but no one gave him anything.

¹⁷ 'When he came to his senses, he said, "How many of my father's hired men have food to spare, and here I am starving to death! ¹⁸ I will set out and go back to my father and say to him: 'Father, I have sinned against heaven and against you. ¹⁹ I am no longer worthy to be called your son; make me like one of your hired men.'" ²⁰ So he got up and went to his father.

'But while he was still a long way off, his father saw him and was filled with compassion for him; he ran to his son, threw his arms around him and kissed him.

²¹ 'The son said to him, "Father, I have sinned against heaven and against you. I am no longer worthy to be called your son."

²² 'But the father said to his servants, "Quick! Bring the best robe and put it on him. Put a ring on his finger and sandals on his feet. ²³ Bring the fattened calf and kill it. Let's have a feast and celebrate. ²⁴ For this son of mine was dead and is alive again; he was lost and is found." So they began to celebrate.

²⁵ 'Meanwhile, the older son was in the field. When he came near the house, he heard music and dancing. ²⁶ So he called one of the servants and asked him what was going on. ²⁷ "Your brother has come," he replied, "and your father has killed the fattened calf because he has him back safe and sound."

²⁸ 'The older brother became angry and refused to go in. So his father went out and pleaded with him. ²⁹ But he

answered his father, "Look! All these years I've been slaving for you and never disobeyed your orders. Yet you never gave me even a young goat so I could celebrate with my friends. [30] But when this son of yours who has squandered your property with prostitutes comes home, you kill the fattened calf for him!"

[31] "'My son,' the father said, "you are always with me, and everything I have is yours. [32]But we had to celebrate and be glad, because this brother of yours was dead and is alive again; he was lost and is found.'"

Luke 15:1–32

Hard words for hard hearts

I am sure your mother told you that it's rude to mutter. But the muttering that we find in Luke 15:2 is not just rude— it is deadly. This muttering, worse than any other kind, was vocalised by the Pharisees and teachers of the law, who said of Jesus: 'This man welcomes sinners and eats with them.' That is the sum and substance of the charge that they brought against Jesus.

Standing accused by their muttering, Jesus defends himself by telling three parables in quick succession, all of which add up to him pleading guilty as charged. 'Yes', he says, 'I do welcome sinners, I do eat with them, and what is more, every time I do the courts of heaven rejoice. In fact, there is more joy in heaven over one sinner who repents than over ninety-nine righteous people who do not need to repent, and God's angels join in.'

Many people reading this book will know of at least one prodigal son who has made his way back into the fold. Perhaps you would count yourself as a prodigal, someone who was interested in God, but who has now moved on. This means that it would be easy for us to focus in on the relationships that we are bound up with as we read these parables. My child, or grandchild, who has wandered away from the fold. My spouse who stopped going to church decades ago. My own situation as a wanderer. The relevance of Jesus' teaching is so striking that we easily fill our minds with comparable situations, but we are less likely to see in our own hearts that elder-brother-spirit. As we read these parables are we actually most like the Pharisees? What if we are the self-righteous, those who are angry at the generosity of God in forgiving sinful people and welcoming no-hopers and outcasts into his family (including the person who hurt me but who now attends worship and claims to be a Christian?). The fact that my goodness seems to count for so little, when someone else, sinful in a hundred ways, can walk in off the street and be accepted. 'This son of yours, who has squandered your property with prostitutes comes home, and you kill the fattened calf for him!' All these years I've been slaving away for you and never disobeyed your orders, and what have you given me? Nothing. Absolutely nothing.

Seeing myself in the elder brother

Jesus taught these parables not to reach the ones who know they are lost, but to burst the bubble of the self-righteous legalists whose pride has blinded them to how far away from the kingdom they are. Jesus told the parables to expose hard hearts to so massive an injection of love that his words might shock people into joy and gladness instead of the more normal fault-finding hypocrisy. Gloomy pretence and a world of religious, smug piety is in for a shock whenever Jesus hears its deadly muttering.

Have you ever found yourself muttering about grace? God's undeserved favour evokes a hostile and bitter reaction in self-righteous hearts. There are, of course, extreme cases of this hostility. A young person becomes a Christian and their joy in Christ is met with bitter resentment in their parents or among their closest friends. They have an instant and violent reaction to any expression of the Christian faith that seems over the top, enthusiastic, or to use the most condemnatory of words, 'fundamentalist'. The parents are not committed

Muslims or even open and convinced atheists. Far from it, they are church goers. They went to Sunday School and are still members of the local church. But their religion is in the same category as eating out, the rotary club and politics—all things in moderation, and probably best not spoken about too often. 'Why, we have a perfectly respectable approach to life and our family has never been one to go in for that kind of thing. We do not mix with the likes of them.'

It's a subtle thing, but as the Pharisees stood and muttered, their resentment of the love that Jesus Christ was showing to others was dressed up as standards, traditions and principles. The Pharisee cannot discern between what lies at the heart of his religion and what is accumulated baggage and tradition. Our muttering is very frightening if we can only step back from it and realise that we would sometimes prefer people to remain outside the kingdom than to enter it.

Just imagine the elder brother in the parable of the lost son. There he is, hard at work in the fields after his younger brother had left with his share of the money. On the outside, of course he looks loyal and diligent, but as he works the ground his heart is self-congratulatory and smug. Does he have one ounce of sympathy for his father in the loss of his son? I doubt it. Too full of his own success, too preoccupied with his own position, too blind to the heartache caused by his younger brother's sin. The seed of his anger is taking root. The seed of proud, self-righteous anger—the attitude which enjoys one's own virtues and despises others' sins—is a seed which grows silently like a cancer until it eventually bursts, as it does at the end of this parable, in an uncontrollable outpouring of rage. Self-righteousness is the breeding ground for deadly muttering, and deadly muttering when full grown is the spiritual equivalent of a terminal disease that leads to the kind of anger that refuses to go in to the party, and sits outside in a huff. So there he sits, as we so often do too.

Seeing myself in the prodigal son

I have to confess: I love the younger son. He has flair, he has plenty of folly as well; but he definitely has flair. He is wild and uncontrolled, full of passion and energy. His crusading zeal doesn't need to be broken and snuffed out, but re-channelled and focused on honouring his father rather than abusing his father's generosity. None of this means, of course, that ending up in the pigsty is preferable. Outside is outside. It doesn't matter if you are away in a foreign land enjoying anonymous sex, gambling and drinking, or whether you are serving the father with a hard heart. Both are forms of life far away from God. Both are a hellish existence.

But when the famine begins, and the lost son ends up feeding pigs (which in Jesus' day was the worst job imaginable), then he begins to take stock. He quickly realises that he has things badly wrong (v. 18). To say 'I am wrong' is one of the few unacceptable attitudes known in our culture. I remember speaking to a young girl who had messed up badly. She had let herself down, her family down, and she had let God down. But she told me the thing she found most difficult was people who tried to tell her that she hadn't done anything wrong.

Can you imagine if some people met the younger son on his way home to the Father, and tried to sit him down? 'Now don't be hard on yourself, you didn't do anything wrong, all you were doing was following your feelings. You were being true to yourself, and you mustn't suppress your desires.' Well, they may have got a black eye, so desperate was this lad to beg his father for mercy and so deep were his convictions about the folly of his sin. He even uttered those unmentionable words (v. 19): 'I am no longer worthy.'

It's hard to repent of sin in a society that tells us we have never sinned. Perhaps you have on occasion taken stock as this boy did and found yourself lost, broken, hopeless, and despairing. Perhaps you have concluded, as he did, that the scale of your folly is too big to contemplate. If so, then no number of voices telling you otherwise will keep you from returning to someone you have hurt and whose love you have spurned. Their acceptance of you is worth a million times all that you have squandered.

So when it comes to God and us, this is where all of heaven's hosts rejoice and where the angels sing. This is where chains of addiction and sin are broken as the lad sets out for home: 'I have sinned against heaven and against you.' Here is repentant love meeting the embrace of the wounded lover and there is no happiness like that in all the world. Forgiveness, restoration, healing and joy all combine in one wonderful homecoming whereby someone who was lost is found. This is unsurpassed happiness.

Recently there was an £85m roll-over in the British National Lottery. Pity the person who won it, and who thought that a paltry helping of passing financial currency is the best they can have. Pity the millions who want to win it and who think they would rather have something other than being reunited with their Creator. Pity you if you are still outside, and still think the embrace of your heavenly Father is worth trading for anything or anyone else.

I have read the printed report from a fire inspector after he visited my house. It's full of long paragraphs of explanation, regulations, and the latest standards. The section at the end reads 'Action to be taken'. This includes three categories: 'Non-essential' (I can ignore that); 'Advised action' (I can ignore that); 'Urgent action required' (I had better act now).

Are you sulking outside the Father's house, slightly bemused at the party going on inside, and slightly indignant at the people who are going into the kingdom of Jesus? Then Jesus' report on your life says, 'Urgent action required'. The invitation is filled with the love and passion of the Father's Son who came from heaven into the far country to find us. He came to seek and to save the lost. He came to wound and to heal the proud.

If you're lost, come home. If you're outside, come in.

8

The Price of Freedom

¹⁴ When the hour came, Jesus and his apostles reclined at the table. ¹⁵ And he said to them, 'I have eagerly desired to eat this Passover with you before I suffer. ¹⁶For I tell you, I will not eat it again until it finds fulfillment in the kingdom of God.'

¹⁷ After taking the cup, he gave thanks and said, 'Take this and divide it among you. ¹⁸ For I tell you I will not drink again of the fruit of the vine until the kingdom of God comes.'

¹⁹ And he took bread, gave thanks and broke it, and gave it to them, saying, 'This is my body given for you; do this in remembrance of me.'

²⁰ In the same way, after the supper he took the cup, saying, 'This cup is the new covenant in my blood, which is poured out for you. ²¹ But the hand of him who is going to betray me is with mine on the table. ²² The Son of Man will go as it has been decreed, but woe to that man who betrays him.' ²³ They began to question among themselves which of them it might be who would do this.

Luke 22:14–23

⁵⁴ Then seizing him, they led him away and took him into the house of the high priest. Peter followed at a distance. ⁵⁵ But when they had kindled a fire in the middle of the courtyard and had sat down together, Peter sat down with them. ⁵⁶ A servant girl saw him seated there in the firelight. She looked closely at him and said, 'This man was with him.'

⁵⁷ But he denied it. 'Woman, I don't know him,' he said.

⁵⁸ A little later someone else saw him and said, 'You also are one of them.'

'Man, I am not!' Peter replied.

⁵⁹ About an hour later another asserted, 'Certainly this fellow was with him, for he is a Galilean.'

⁶⁰ Peter replied, 'Man, I don't know what you're talking about!' Just as he was speaking, the rooster crowed. ⁶¹ The Lord turned and looked straight at Peter. Then Peter remembered the word the Lord had spoken to him: 'Before the rooster crows today, you will disown me three times.' ⁶² And he went outside and wept bitterly.

⁶³ The men who were guarding Jesus began mocking and beating him. ⁶⁴ They blindfolded him and demanded, 'Prophesy! Who hit you?' ⁶⁵ And they said many other insulting things to him.

⁶⁶ At daybreak the council of the elders of the people, both the chief priests and teachers of the law, met together, and Jesus was led before them. ⁶⁷ 'If you are the Christ,' they said, 'tell us.'

Jesus answered, 'If I tell you, you will not believe me, ⁶⁸ and if I asked you, you would not answer. ⁶⁹ But from now on, the Son of Man will be seated at the right hand of the mighty God.'

⁷⁰ They all asked, 'Are you then the Son of God?'

He replied, 'You are right in saying I am.'

⁷¹ Then they said, 'Why do we need any more testimony? We have heard it from his own lips.'

23 ¹ Then the whole assembly rose and led him off to Pilate. ² And they began to accuse him, saying, 'We have found this man subverting our nation. He opposes

payment of taxes to Caesar and claims to be Christ, a king.'

³ So Pilate asked Jesus, 'Are you the king of the Jews?'

'Yes, it is as you say,' Jesus replied.

⁴ Then Pilate announced to the chief priests and the crowd, 'I find no basis for a charge against this man.'

⁵ But they insisted, 'He stirs up the people all over Judea by his teaching. He started in Galilee and has come all the way here.'

⁶ On hearing this, Pilate asked if the man was a Galilean. ⁷ When he learned that Jesus was under Herod's jurisdiction, he sent him to Herod, who was also in Jerusalem at that time.

⁸ When Herod saw Jesus, he was greatly pleased, because for a long time he had been wanting to see him. From what he had heard about him, he hoped to see him perform some miracle. ⁹ He plied him with many questions, but Jesus gave him no answer. ¹⁰ The chief priests and the teachers of the law were standing there, vehemently accusing him. ¹¹ Then Herod and his soldiers ridiculed and mocked him. Dressing him in an elegant robe, they sent him back to Pilate. ¹² That day Herod and Pilate became friends—before this they had been enemies.

¹³ Pilate called together the chief priests, the rulers and the people, ¹⁴ and said to them, 'You brought me this man as one who was inciting the people to rebellion. I have examined him in your presence and have found no basis for your charges against him. ¹⁵ Neither has Herod, for he sent him back to us; as you can see, he has done nothing to deserve death. ¹⁶ Therefore, I will punish him and then release him.'

¹⁸ With one voice they cried out, 'Away with this man! Release Barabbas to us!' ¹⁹ (Barabbas had been thrown into prison for an insurrection in the city, and for murder.)

²⁰ Wanting to release Jesus, Pilate appealed to them again. ²¹ But they kept shouting, 'Crucify him! Crucify him!'

²² For the third time he spoke to them: 'Why? What crime has this man committed? I have found in him no grounds for the death penalty. Therefore I will have him punished and then release him.'

²³ But with loud shouts they insistently demanded that he be crucified, and their shouts prevailed. ²⁴ So Pilate decided to grant their demand. ²⁵ He released the man who had been thrown into prison for insurrection and murder, the one they asked for, and surrendered Jesus to their will.

²⁶ As they led him away, they seized Simon from Cyrene, who was on his way in from the country, and put the cross on him and made him carry it behind Jesus. ²⁷ A large number of people followed him, including women who mourned and wailed for him. ²⁸ Jesus turned and said to them, 'Daughters of Jerusalem, do not weep for me; weep for yourselves and for your children. ²⁹ For the time will come when you will say, "Blessed are the barren women, the wombs that never bore and the breasts that never nursed!" ³⁰ Then they will say to the mountains, "Fall on us!" and to the hills, "Cover us!" ³¹ For if men do these things when the tree is green, what will happen when it is dry?'

³² Two other men, both criminals, were also led out with him to be executed. ³³ When they came to the place called the Skull, there they crucified him, along with the criminals—one on his right, the other on his left. ³⁴ Jesus said, 'Father, forgive them, for they do not know what they are doing.' And they divided up his clothes by casting lots.

³⁵ The people stood watching, and the rulers even sneered at him. They said, 'He saved others; let him save himself if he is the Christ of God, the Chosen One.'

³⁶ The soldiers also came up and mocked him. They offered him wine vinegar ³⁷ and said, 'If you are the king of the Jews, save yourself.'

³⁸ There was a written notice above him, which read: THIS IS THE KING OF THE JEWS.

³⁹ One of the criminals who hung there hurled insults at him: 'Aren't you the Christ? Save yourself and us!'

⁴⁰ But the other criminal rebuked him. 'Don't you fear God,' he said, 'since you are under the same sentence? ⁴¹ We are punished justly, for we are getting what our deeds deserve. But this man has done nothing wrong.'

⁴²Then he said, 'Jesus, remember me when you come into your kingdom.'

⁴³Jesus answered him, 'I tell you the truth, today you will be with me in paradise.'

⁴⁴It was now about the sixth hour, and darkness came over the whole land until the ninth hour, ⁴⁵for the sun stopped shining. And the curtain of the temple was torn in two. ⁴⁶Jesus called out with a loud voice, 'Father, into your hands I commit my spirit.' When he had said this, he breathed his last.

⁴⁷The centurion, seeing what had happened, praised God and said, 'Surely this was a righteous man.' ⁴⁸When all the people who had gathered to witness this sight saw what took place, they beat their breasts and went away. ⁴⁹But all those who knew him, including the women who had followed him from Galilee, stood at a distance, watching these things.

Luke 22:54–23:49

A cruel and sadistic deity?

On 1st April 2009, sixteen oil industry workers lost their lives in a tragic helicopter accident in the North Sea, not far from the Aberdeen coastline. They were returning home from the rigs to their family and friends. Several people in our church work in this industry, and some in our church knew at least one of those who died. The whole city was shaken by such terrible loss of life. There was a tangible sense of fear and foreboding for those continuing to commute off-shore for their work.

Not long after this accident came Easter, with the usual Good Friday service in our church. I was struck by an acute contrast. Having been confronted with death and bitter pain, here we were now, in church, reading about the violent, agonising death of an innocent man, but doing so with glad and thankful hearts. Jesus suffered the indignity of being spat on, punched and slapped, as well as the flayed skin of scourging and the brutality of a Roman crucifixion. Large nails pierced the bones in his hands and feet, followed by slow suffocation as his body weight pressed down on his lungs. Yet instead of thinking of this as a tragedy, Christians say that the death of Jesus is the greatest and most amazing event in the history of the world.

Of course, not everyone agrees. Some have picked up on the incongruity between the way we think about death generally and the way Christians think about the death of Jesus in particular. Richard Dawkins writes:

> I have described [Jesus' death on the cross for sin], the central doctrine of Christianity as vicious, sadomasochistic and repellent. We should also dismiss it as barking mad, but for its familiarity with which it has dulled our objectivity. If God wanted to forgive our sins, why not just forgive them, without having himself tortured and executed in payment.
>
> *The God Delusion* (London: Bantam, 2006), 253.

Dawkins' point is simple. If we stop and think about the way Jesus died, then reverent awe will give way to repulsion and disgust. This objection rests on the normal way people react to the tragedy of death and it raises an important question: what kind of God would send his Son to suffer a violent death at the hands of wicked men? But more than this, Dawkins' words cut right to the heart of the driving argument of this book. We have seen Jesus proclaim good news to the bankrupt, we have seen him cancel the debts of the guilty, and give to the destitute and outcast the riches of a relationship with God. So hadn't Jesus done everything he said he came to do? Surely he had been wiping people's debts away and providing forgiveness without ever having to go to the cross? Why did he have to die?

In this chapter I want to focus on three facets of Jesus' death that put the pieces of this puzzle together: his blood, his trial, and his death. Taken together, they explain why Christians remember the day that Jesus died as Good Friday. These three aspects of Christ's death will then lead us to consider the significance of the resurrection, the claim that Jesus rose from the dead.

His blood, my forgiveness

However distasteful it may seem to us, the Gospel writers are interested in blood—and Luke is no exception. One verse printed at the start of this chapter sheds light on everything that follows. As Jesus and his disciples celebrate the Passover, Jesus takes the cup, and as his disciples are drinking from it he tells them: 'This cup is the new covenant in my blood, which is poured out for you' (Luke 22:20).

Hours before his death, sitting round a table celebrating the Passover, Jesus is explaining what his death means. As he dies and his blood is shed, it will be the blood of a 'new covenant'. The word 'covenant' means an unbreakable promise of close relationship. To be in covenant with someone is to be bound to them in the closest possible way. The disciples knew this because the Passover feast itself celebrated God's covenant with his people in Old Testament times. It reminded them of how God rescued them from Egypt and bound them to himself as his people. Once the people were rescued from Egypt, God made a new covenant with them, namely that he would be their God and they would be his people. Even as this new relationship was forged, the people said 'We will do everything the LORD has said, we will obey'. As they spoke these words, an animal lay dead, its blood poured on the altar and sprinkled on the people (Exod. 24:1–8). Why the gore when a covenant is made? Why the bloodshed when God comes to be in relationship with his people? It is because for God to welcome me into his family there is a cost.

What happens when God says: 'I want to be in the closest possible relationship with you'? The God who is perfect and holy and who cannot tolerate sin for a second, how can this God be united to me in covenant love? You might not want to know me if everything I have said, thought or done were listed for you on paper. You certainly would not know where to look were I to tell you face to face. So if we feel such shame about ourselves, the question is: how does a God of absolute purity say to us: 'You are mine. I love you. I want you to be with me forever'? There is only one way God can do that, and that is if all my shame, guilt, and sin is paid for. Only if the cost of my sin is met can that relationship happen.

Dawkins asks the question: 'If God wanted to forgive why not just forgive, why the need for payment?' In saying this, he expects from God what we would not expect from anyone else. Some years ago a young woman was brutally murdered. Her father said that his life had been smashed into tiny pieces. 'Since our daughter's death,' he said, 'we have experienced the blinding need for her killer to be caught and for punishment to be handed out.' Punishment is part of how the world is made. We react against evil, we want justice. But if that is what we are like, then what must evil look like to God? The woman's father was crying out for justice in a way that Dawkins implies is 'repellent'. In contrast, what we learn from Jesus' death is that God does not over-ride or ignore the need for justice. For me to be forgiven and be close to God there is a cost, a price—and the price is the punishment of my sin. The only suitable punishment is death. This is why the Bible describes blood being shed. Jesus' blood is shed as his life is taken in punishment for my sin. His blood shed instead of mine means that my sins are forgiven and I am cleansed. The price has been paid. It's a wonderful picture of what God does for sinners whom he loves.

Can you remember what it was like to be a child, in the days before you became conscious of dirt, and you were outside in the garden, the mud, the rain and the puddles and you were covered in dirt from top to toe? Then it was time to go inside and as you stood at the door with your mother's lovely cream carpet stretching ahead of you, you felt a hand holding you just as you were about to take off at high speed in your boots: 'Hang on, not like this you don't!' And you were stripped down and scrubbed clean, all the dirt washed off, and you were dressed in clean clothes.

When Jesus says 'this is my blood of the covenant' he is saying 'I am going to join you to me as a bride is joined to her husband. You can join my family, you can enter my kingdom and be at my side. But you're dirty. You need to be washed. My blood will do that. It's poured out to wash away sins because I know you need it. Your guilt has kept you awake at night. You've woken early with a heavy heart because of it. You keep replaying the scene a thousand times in your mind, and you would do anything to take back what you said and undo what you did—but you can't. Your shame feels like dirt that you cannot get rid of. So drink from my cup. I can wash you. I can make you clean. Had your sins been printed on paper the page would now be white, they would be gone. You never need to carry around in your heart the price of your sin, because my blood has been shed and you can be forgiven.'

His trial, my freedom

If Jesus' blood needed to be shed, did it matter how he died? It's an important question. If Jesus had been murdered by thieves along a roadside, or slain in a violent uprising in Jerusalem, or any other way we could think of, would the effects of his death be the same? Perhaps the only important thing is that blood is shed and it does not matter how.

But Luke prevents us thinking that this was a possible remedy. The drama of the narrative shows us that the events which led to Christ's death contain vital clues about its meaning. In a reading of the Gospels it's easy to make the mistake of seeing the incidents leading up to Jesus' death as merely side events along the way to the main event; simply the things that happened to seal his fate. But they are much more than that. Luke skilfully constructs his narrative to show us that as Jesus goes to his death several people are on trial. First, we see Peter, one of Jesus' disciples tested and tried as to whether he is a follower of Jesus. He fails the test. Then comes Jesus' trial before his own people and Pilate, and here Luke paints a deliberate picture. Jesus is innocent, and his prosecutors are guilty; but Jesus is treated as if he is guilty, and they act as if they are innocent. By writing in this way Luke even turns the tables on us, his readers. Let's look more closely at how he does this.

Peter is Jesus' big, bold disciple. He leads with his feet, full of bravado, passion and commitment. Peter tells Jesus that he is ready to go with him 'to prison and to death' (Luke 22:33); Jesus tells Peter that instead 'you will deny three times that you know me' (22:34). When the crunch comes, and Peter is questioned three times about whether he is a follower of Jesus, exactly as Jesus had prophesied, Peter denies all knowledge of him. As Peter weeps, realising Jesus' prediction had come true, Jesus is being beaten and mocked and asked to prophecy. Luke wants the irony to have a profound effect on us. The very thing Jesus has done for Peter is the very thing he is asked to do by the soldiers. Their guilt now follows Peter's guilt, for they cannot see who they are insulting. The guilt of the soldiers is followed by the guilt of the chief priests and the teachers of the law as they refuse to believe Jesus' revelation of who he is. But most telling of all is the climax of his trial before Pilate.

'Are you the King of the Jews?', Pilate asks him.

'Yes.'

The conversation leads Pilate to realise that there is no basis for any charges against Jesus. But he is weak. He is cowardly. Despite his statement that Jesus 'has done nothing to deserve death' (23:15), Pilate gives in to the blood-thirsty mob and signs the death warrant of an innocent man.

Notice what is happening here. Guilty men try an innocent man and find him not guilty, yet still they sentence him to death. They act as if they are innocent and try the innocent as if he is guilty. By weaving the account together like this, Luke shows that in the courtroom an incredible swap takes place. The details of what happens historically to all the main characters in the courtroom create a picture of what happens spiritually to those who come to see who Jesus is and who trust him for forgiveness. The guilty live and go free; the innocent dies. It's the courtroom drama that shows us that a transfer of condemnation takes place. The one person who deserved to go free, the only person who deserved to live, is led out to die.

As he records the historical facts, Luke paints a picture to show us that we cannot stand and watch this courtroom drama from the gallery. We cannot look on from the sidelines without realising that we should be in the dock; we should be condemned, not Jesus. This means that you and I cannot look closely at Jesus without realising that his innocence is so clear that it sheds great beams of light onto our guilt. So much so that we realise Luke's point here is this: who is actually on trial? Jesus is standing there, but who is being weighed in the balance? Peter? The chief priests? Pilate? You? Me? As we look on, stand in the courtroom and hear the sentence being passed, we should realise that our guilt has been placed on Jesus' innocent shoulders.

If we stop to think about our guilt, stare at it and turn it over in our minds, its weight can be crippling. But for some of us the problem is worse when we think of Christ's innocence. It is possible to be wrongly paralysed by guilt and shame as we think about Jesus dying as an innocent man in the place of the guilty. The BBC used to have a Religious Affairs Correspondent called Gerald Priestland who had a radio show called 'Priestland's Progress'. On one show he said that by the time he was ten years old he thought Christianity was all about sin, by the time he was fifteen he was glimpsing the abyss of depression, and describing the next thirty years he said, 'every time I looked at the cross with its suffering victim its only message to me was you did this, and there is no health in you.'

Priestland was partly right. Part of reading about the cross in Luke's Gospel is realising the truth of those words: we did this. I did this. He bears my guilt. But what we read about next is so important. There is a further twist in Luke's courtroom drama. It was the Roman Governor's custom at Passover to release a prisoner chosen by the crowd. On this occasion they had a notorious prisoner in custody called Barabbas, imprisoned for insurrection and murder.

Pilate asks: 'Which of the two do you want me to release to you—Barabbas or Jesus?'

'Barabbas', they answered. 'Crucify Jesus and give us Barabbas!'

So Pilate releases Barabbas to them, but Jesus is flogged and handed over to be crucified.

Just think about what Luke is showing us. The guilt is shared by all as Jesus dies: disciples, Christ's own nation (chief priests and Bible-believing teachers), the pagan world of Roman rulers, you and me. But Luke does not want us to admire Jesus as he dies an innocent man, like a hero in an action movie, or a martyr for a great religious cause. He does not want to leave us lost in our guilt and shame as we see Jesus die an innocent man. It was not for our pity that Jesus died; it was for our immunity, for our freedom. Three crosses hung on the skyline that day and one of them had Barabbas' name all over it. He was on death row. He was a guilty man, destined to die and he deserved it. Yet he walked free, as Jesus took his place. Here's how someone has imagined what it must have been like for Barabbas:

> The yelling of the crowds grew ever louder. Barabbas couldn't hear everything, but the few phrases he did manage to pick out froze his blood: 'We want Barabbas!' 'Crucify him! Crucify him!' This is it, he thought. Not long now and it will all be over.
>
> There were footsteps approaching outside in the corridor.

Barabbas felt his stomach muscles tense involuntarily and a sudden nausea overwhelm him as the bolts of the cell door were drawn back. As the door opened he muttered a quick prayer under his breath. Old habits refused to die.

What happened next took several minutes to sink in. Surely there must be some mistake. He repeated the guard's words to himself: 'All right, Barabbas, you can go. You're a free man. Don't ask me why, but they're going to crucify Jesus of Nazareth instead of you.'

> Richard Bauckham and Trevor Hart, *At the Cross: Meditations on People Who Were There* (London: Darton, Longman and Todd Ltd, 1999), 66.

'You did this. You did this—but you're a free man.' That's what Gerald Priestland could have heard. That's what Luke says to us as we see Jesus taken out to die. Get up. Walk free. You can go. It is a staggering thing to be told. To be someone who Jesus loves is to be a person who is left wondering what to do with the rest of a life that we did not expect or deserve to have.

I do not know what your most awful shame is or the memories that bring the guilt flooding back; I know mine, but because Jesus died these things have nothing to contribute to my future. They are gone, finished, done away with: and I have in front of me a life I did not deserve to have. So stare at the cross—look hard and look long. But once you have looked, turn and live. Christ is led out to die, while the people he loves and dies for are set free.

His death, my life

Each of these different themes receive their clearest expression as we read some of Jesus' final words. Now nailed to the cross, he is hanging between two 'criminals' on crosses, one on either side. The translation 'criminal' doesn't tell us everything—more likely they were there for the same sort of crimes as Barabbas, perhaps for being violent revolutionaries waging guerrilla warfare on the occupying forces of the Roman army. One of them joins in heaping mockery and vitriol on Jesus as he dies: 'Aren't you the Christ? Save yourself and us.' But the other criminal sees the reality of what is happening: 'We are being punished justly, for we are getting what our sins deserve. But this man has done nothing wrong.'

Given everything we have seen of Jesus' compassion for the poor, the marginalised and the outcast in Luke's Gospel, it is no surprise that now, as he dies, Jesus once again wipes away one sinner's debts and welcomes him into his family: 'I tell you the truth,' Jesus said to this criminal, 'today you will be with me in paradise.'

Luke is not content simply to show us Jesus taking the place of the guilty as he dies; he wants us to see Jesus granting life to the guilty as he dies. If the price of our freedom is Jesus' death on the cross, then the way to experience that freedom is simply to look to Jesus and ask for his mercy. That is all the dying man said: 'Jesus, remember me when you come into your kingdom.' The plea for mercy comes from a man who knows he does not deserve it and who knows that what he does deserve is the agony he is now experiencing on the cross. What he hears as he dies is good news for the poor, freedom for the prisoner, favour for the guilty, life for the dying and welcome for the outcast. By asking for mercy from Jesus we receive eternity with Jesus.

His life, my future

In Luke 24, we read the astonishing claim that after being placed in a sealed and guarded tomb, the body of Jesus Christ was raised again to life. The first visitors to the tomb, coming to anoint the body with spices, were women (interestingly, unlike our society today, not the gender of witnesses you would choose in the first century if you wanted to make up an incredible story to be passed off as fact). Instead of finding Jesus' body, they find an empty tomb and an angel who says to them: 'Remember how Jesus told you, while he was still with you in Galilee: "The Son of Man must be delivered into the hands of sinful men, be crucified and on the third day be raised again." Then they remembered his words' (Luke 24:6).

Just as when Jesus' birth was announced and explained by angelic messengers, so now his death and resurrection is explained as the fulfilment of earlier teaching—this time, his own teaching. Three times in Luke's Gospel Jesus is recorded as having predicted in precise detail the nature of his death and the timing of his resurrection. As these women see the empty tomb and two angels, they almost collapse with fright and fear. But when they hear the angels' words the picture falls into place. They remember what Jesus had promised, and immediately go to tell the other disciples everything that happened. The central message of the angels' words is that Jesus had predicted and embraced the agony of his death. Jesus' words about his death are recalled because his death had been his reason for coming into the world in the first place.

When the women bowed down in front of the angels at the empty tomb, it is striking that what the angels gave them was not a piece of Jesus' grave clothes for them to touch, nor a drop of his blood to bless them, but the words Jesus had taught to change them. This is real and practical for us. Everything about the way we naturally think, and everything about the culture we live in—and sadly plenty of things about the priorities and language of churches today—leads us to believe that something other than Jesus' words will bring us the light and help we need. Today people will queue for miles in Jerusalem to touch the empty tomb in the church of the Holy Sepulchre, and what they do not realise is that what they desperately need is not to touch but to hear. It is not the things we see that transform our lives, it is the words we listen to.

What is it exactly that they hear in these words: 'The Son of Man must be delivered into the hands of sinful men, be crucified and on the third day be raised again'? What they hear is that everything has changed if Jesus is alive. Everything the women had ever thought about who Jesus was, everything they had ever thought about life and death was turned on its head as the light dawned in their hearts: death is not what we thought it was, it is not the end.

If you were a first-century Jew, you were waiting for God to act decisively in history. You were waiting to be set free from the tyrannical might of Rome; you were waiting for the king who would bring in a new creation. You were longing for the king who would make everything sad in the world come untrue, the king who would destroy death itself, raise people from the dead and restore them to life with God in a world made new. That was your hope, your greatest desire. You were waiting for the new world to dawn.

In Austria, in 1984, Joseph Fritzl imprisoned his daughter in a cellar under his house. He fathered children by her, some of whom died, some of whom he introduced to the outside world, but three of whom lived in that cellar without ever seeing daylight. All they knew were the narrow corridors and low ceilings of their dungeon world. As far as they were concerned, this was life. This was how everyone lives. This was the world and there wasn't anything else.

Imagine what it was like for those children when Fritzl was caught and they were freed. Of course there would be all sorts of problems introducing them to the real world. But, if that process was handled well and carefully, think what their new life would be like. Think of a child discovering that beaches and oceans really do exist. Feeling the sand and the water; tasting coke, ice-cream and hamburgers; playing with toys, cars and dolls. Think of the best things that would ever thrill a child's heart and imagine the feeling as the new world dawned on their lives. That is what happened on the day of the resurrection for the women and for all the disciples. It wasn't just that the Jesus they loved was alive, rather, the way they viewed the world, the confines of their lives had been shattered forever.

We are born, we grow, we live, we work, we grow old, we die, some in happiness and prosperity, others in hardship and poverty, and as we live we think: this is it. Seventy years, if we're lucky—then the end. So we live in the cellar, our vision blinkered, our growth stunted, unless we see that a new world is coming. It's coming.

But how do we know? How do we know that one day the dead will be raised, that the body placed in the grave will rise to stand before Almighty God? How do we know that one day all our suffering will end, that God's tender hand will wipe away all our tears? How can I possibly believe that when it hurts so much here and now? The answer to all these questions is: the resurrection of Jesus Christ. The resurrection of Jesus is God's promise of a new world given in advance while we live in the old world.

We know what it's like when we have made our summer holiday arrangements. There may be some weeks of work and stress still to come, but there's no going back. We're heading towards the rest we need. And so it is with death. Still it is with us, but Christ's resurrection stands alone in history as the evidence that death's stranglehold has been broken and that a new world, the world we long for, is coming.

I hope by now that one simple point has been coming through loud and clear in the pages of this book. Luke addresses you as you read these pages. Take all the problems of your life, he says, and all the mistakes of your past. Take all the temptations that grip your soul, and all the times that you have fallen, and fallen and fallen again. Take all the shame that you feel and the guilt that you carry, all the accusing voices from inside and from outside that tell you a hundred times a day that there is no one who is for you and no one who can set you free. Take all the anger of God whose holiness and love you have violated and whose goodness you have scorned; all the standards you have smashed and the commands that lie in smithereens around your feet—take it all and place it on the innocent shoulders of Jesus and let him pay for it for you. Take all your fear of dying and your sorrow and grief, which lives with you every day because of the spectre of death that has wreaked havoc in your life and the lives of those you love. Bring it all to the empty tomb of Jesus Christ where death lies dead, a promise and a foretaste of what is to come.

No longer bankrupt, you have become rich. You can now go free.

9

The Big Picture

[14]Jesus returned to Galilee in the power of the Spirit, and news about him spread through the whole countryside. [15]He taught in their synagogues, and everyone praised him.

[16]He went to Nazareth, where he had been brought up, and on the Sabbath day he went into the synagogue, as was his custom. And he stood up to read. [17]The scroll of the prophet Isaiah was handed to him. Unrolling it, he found the place where it is written:

> [18] The Spirit of the Lord is on me,
>   because he has anointed me
>   to preach good news to the poor.
> He has sent me to proclaim freedom for the prisoners
>   and recovery of sight for the blind,
> to release the oppressed,
>   [19]to proclaim the year of the Lord's favour.

[20]Then he rolled up the scroll, gave it back to the attendant and sat down. The eyes of everyone in the synagogue were fastened on him, [21]and he began by saying to them, 'Today this scripture is fulfilled in your hearing.'

[22]All spoke well of him and were amazed at the gracious words that came from his lips. 'Isn't this Joseph's son?' they asked.

²³ Jesus said to them, 'Surely you will quote this proverb to me: "Physician, heal yourself! Do here in your hometown what we have heard that you did in Capernaum."'

²⁴ 'I tell you the truth,' he continued, 'no prophet is accepted in his hometown. ²⁵ I assure you that there were many widows in Israel in Elijah's time, when the sky was shut for three and a half years and there was a severe famine throughout the land. ²⁶ Yet Elijah was not sent to any of them, but to a widow in Zarephath in the region of Sidon. ²⁷ And there were many in Israel with leprosy in the time of Elisha the prophet, yet not one of them was cleansed—only Naaman the Syrian.'

²⁸ All the people in the synagogue were furious when they heard this. ²⁹ They got up, drove him out of the town, and took him to the brow of the hill on which the town was built, in order to throw him down the cliff. ³⁰ But he walked right through the crowd and went on his way.

Luke 4:14–30

It's not over until it's over

In this final chapter we're going to go back to where we started: Jesus in the synagogue in Nazareth. That's where we left Jesus in chapter one, having announced his manifesto to rapturous applause. He is the one who has come to proclaim the year of the Lord's favour, to bring good news to the poor and freedom for the oppressed—and that's exactly what we have seen him do throughout this book.

But in chapter one we only looked at half the story. The Nazareth congregation start off admiring Jesus for what he had to say, but by the end of Luke 4 they have become so enraged at Jesus that they take him to the edge of a cliff to get rid of him for good. In this final chapter, I want to look at what Jesus said that led the people to turn against him so quickly and so violently. This brings us full circle in the book to see that, in essence, there are only ever two ways to respond to Jesus as he offers us his good news.

Question-time

The first hint that things are about to turn ugly appears in 4:22. It's just a small sign, but it explains why Jesus begins to probe his seemingly adoring listeners: 'All spoke well of Jesus and were amazed at the gracious words that came from his lips. 'Isn't this Joseph's son?' they asked. It seems an innocent question. What Jesus perceives in this inquiry, however, is that the congregation are impressed with the preaching but they are not so sure about the preacher. 'This is great stuff—but surely Jesus can't be talking about himself, can he? This is the boy next door speaking. We've seen him grow up, we know his parents, he's a local lad. Is he really going to be the one to carry out all these incredible acts of liberation?'

In and of itself, of course, questioning Jesus is never a bad thing. I have written this book because I believe that to explore Jesus' identity and the claims he made about himself and his mission is one of the most important things you can ever do. Was he only a figure in history? Was he just a carpenter? A prophet? A wise teacher? Seeking answers to such questions is essential and Luke himself wrote his Gospel to help a friend (Theophilus) who needed to be sure of the answers. But there is all the difference in the world between the questioning of a sincere seeker and the questioning of a cynical sceptic. Jesus discerns that in the synagogue he is faced with the latter group and so he pre-empts their next move. 'Surely you will quote this proverb to me: "Physician, heal yourself! Do here in your hometown what we have heard that you did in Capernaum"' (4:23). Jesus has just said that he has come to bring freedom, to bring recovery of sight, to release the oppressed and he realises his listeners are thinking, 'Well, let's see it then. If you've come to do those things, then do them! Then we'll believe that you're not just a local lad with grand pretensions!'

That kind of response to Jesus is widespread. I often hear people say, 'I would believe in your Jesus if I could see him with my own eyes, or if I could see him do a miracle. It's all very well reading about him in the pages of a book but I've got no real evidence to believe in him.' It may come as a surprise, but Jesus judges this to be the stance of a cynic, regardless of how sincere it sounds. That is because the person making this statement has worked out their own criteria for evaluating Jesus, and is therefore never ready to receive Jesus' evaluation of them. It's a back to front position. It's the wrong way round. The right question to ask is: What do you make of me, Jesus? If I know I need Jesus I will take him at his word. If I think I do not need him, I will set him little tasks to see if he can prove himself before I decide to follow him.

Throughout all four Gospels, Jesus performs miracle after miracle; he is not slow to show God's goodness and power to our broken world. At the same time, he always resists those who come to him looking for miracles as evidence so that they can believe him. That is because to believe in Jesus for what he can do will nearly always obscure the greater reason to believe in Jesus—to believe in him for what he says. When Jesus speaks he reveals who he is, he explains why he came, he makes plain why we need him. If we do not believe in him for those reasons then we might well believe in a Jesus who is powerful but we will always want to treat him like a genie in a lamp. He will be there to do what we say, when we give the word, and as often as we want. In Luke 4, Jesus shows us that he never responds to that way of thinking about him because it is an exercise in getting hold of the wrong end of the stick.

Knowing me, knowing you

Now what that meant in Luke 4 was this. His synagogue listeners sat hanging on his every word, thinking that everything they were hearing was wonderful. Imagine a reporter from 'The Galilee Globe' interrupting the proceedings with his microphone. 'Now, Mr Israelite, are you pleased that your debts are going to be wiped out? How do you feel about being able to see again, and about being released from captivity?'

'Oh', he would say, 'You don't understand—he's not talking to me. We have no debts in our house but lots of people do, so this is all good news. It's part of our tradition, of course, the cancelling of debts, so for those who need it this should be just the kind of pick-me-up they need in these difficult times.'

It is so easy to hear Jesus speaking about setting people free but to miss the fact that I am the one who needs to be set free. It is comforting to listen to words about a fresh start, and the cancelling of debts, without ever grasping that I am the one who is massively in debt. It is easy to spend some free time reading a book about Jesus giving sight to the blind without ever realising that I am the one who is blind. That is what happened that day in the synagogue. It is precisely the reason things turned nasty. All these words coming from Jesus sounded lovely. The natural next step seemed to be to ask him to prove he could do it. But in the cynicism of their words Jesus perceived a hardness in their hearts, which revealed that his listeners did not think his words applied to them. These people were the ones Jesus had come for. They were the ones he had come to set free, to release, to make whole; it was their debts he had come to cancel. Instead, they just sit and listen. 'I wonder when he's going to start doing all this. The people who need it are certainly going to be happy – so long as he can back up his claims. Can he?'

When Jesus tells them that he is not going to give them any miracles to substantiate his claims, things begin to come unstuck. Ironically, by refusing to accept Jesus, his listeners simply prove his point; they reveal themselves to be blind, calloused, and desperately in need of the rescue that he came to bring. But they cannot see it. There's a little play on words in 4:19, which is obscured in our English translations. Jesus says that he has come to proclaim the year of the Lord's 'favour'. The word translated as 'favour' also appears in 4:24 where Jesus says that no prophet is 'accepted' in his home town. God is willing to show his favour, his acceptance, to everyone who is in need; but the people who are in need will not favour Jesus. God will accept people; but the people will not accept God.

The situation begins to get serious. Jesus now gives his listeners a history lesson to show them how dangerous it is to relate to him in this way. He has just classed himself as a rejected prophet, and so he reminds them what happened to Elijah and Elisha, two other rejected prophets in Israel's history (4:25-7):

> I assure you that there were many widows in Israel in Elijah's time, when the sky was shut for three and a half years and there was a severe famine throughout the land. Yet Elijah was not sent to any of them, but to a widow in Zarephath in the region of Sidon. And there were many in Israel with leprosy in the time of Elisha the prophet, yet not one of them was cleansed—only Naaman the Syrian.

The crowd's fury explodes. So what has Jesus just said? His listeners knew that Elijah and Elisha were prophets at times of great unbelief and unfaithfulness on the part of God's people, the nation of Israel. They were prophets when Israel had turned its back on God, they had scorned the covenant God had made with them, and so God responded by 'shutting the sky'— there was no rain and no food for three and a half years. The nation was under divine judgment. Not only did God respond by removing the people's food, he also removed their direct contact with him: the prophets. There were many needy people in Israel during this time (widows and lepers), but God did not send the prophets to help them. Instead God sent his prophets to widows and lepers outside Israel. God sent his prophets to Gentiles while his own people, the Jews, languished in their rebellion. He sent his prophets to people who knew they were in need and who would receive his help with open arms.

Notice what Jesus has just said about himself and what he has just said about his listeners. By identifying himself with Elijah and Elisha, Jesus is saying that God is going to send him away from the people of Israel to people who will listen to him, to Gentiles. By identifying his listeners with unbelieving, unfaithful Israel, Jesus has said his listeners are going to be like the poor and needy, the widows and lepers, who God left without help because they refused to turn to him and call on him for forgiveness. It is a stunning indictment. 'Look,' Jesus is saying, 'remember your history: if you reject the prophet, then God will reject you by sending him instead to people who know that they need him. It happened in Elijah's day. It happened in Elisha's day. And it will happen again today.' As he spoke, his hearers' blood began to boil. How dare Jesus compare them to the widows and lepers in unbelieving Israel! How dare Jesus say that God was concerned for the outcasts and the rejected in the despised Gentile world!

It is like the three nephews of a wealthy spinster aunt who gather in the lawyer's office after they have dutifully attended her funeral. Inwardly they are licking their lips. They have already booked their posh holiday and put down the deposit on their new-build luxury villa. But of course they gather in respectable silence, impeccably dressed in their dark suits. The lawyer opens the envelope and reads out the will. The estate, a million pounds, has been left to the poor little boy who lived down the road from her. Worst of all, he had stolen a heap of money from the old lady and been caught in the act but she had always refused to press charges. He didn't have a penny to his name but once a fortnight he would ring her bell and sit and talk to her for a while. He never had anything to give her. But they became firm friends, and now he was a beneficiary. The nephews are livid. But what can they say? They hadn't been in touch with their aunt for decades but she was still their relative, not his. How dare she include that little nobody in her will! What an outrage that he should be included!

The good people of Nazareth feel like that when they hear Jesus say he has come for the Gentiles of all people, while they are described as helpless widows and lepers in Israel. But, Jesus insists, this is his mission. It is explosive. It is a staggering fact to realise that one of the effects Jesus had on people was to make them so angry that they wanted to kill him. But Luke shows us that the real Jesus is always capable of making people angry because he says to them 'I am your only hope – if you reject me, God will reject you.'

Maybe, on second thoughts, it isn't so surprising that Jesus can make people very angry. The more I think about it, this is always what happens when comfortable, contented people who think they are fine and healthy are told that they are sick and in need of a doctor. It's cliff time. Of course, it's rare that I ever experience this as exploding fury or blind rage. Usually it's just a polite smile or a firm handshake, which gently pushes Jesus to one side and resolutely keeps him at arm's length. That is what happens week in and week out in churches across the land as people hear Jesus speak and assume he cannot be talking to them. Me–blind? Me–bankrupt? Me–destitute? No, no, no–I assume Jesus is talking about someone else. It must be Mrs Jones down the road. Everyone knows what her daughter has been up to and we know why she turned out that way. It must be the poor in the developing world, the destitute where disaster has struck, those who need justice, the marginalised. But not me.

I hope the penny has begun to drop as you've read the pages of this book. As you come to the end of it, if you feel that the people we have met who encountered Jesus are nothing like you, then I would not be surprised if this last chapter makes you angry. If you do not think Jesus has been addressing you then I would understand if you do not want to listen to his words of warning. When someone thinks they do not need Jesus, all they are doing is simply confirming Jesus' judgment of their poverty and debt while remaining blind to it themselves. The danger of rejecting Jesus is real. It means that our rejection of him will one day seal his rejection of us.

At the start of this chapter are printed the words which Jesus quoted from the prophet Isaiah: 'to proclaim the year of the Lord's favour' (Luke 4:19). But in fact Jesus stops midway through Isaiah's sentence. Isaiah continues: 'and the day of vengeance of our God' (Isa. 61:2). By stopping where he does and leaving that sentence out, Jesus is not leaving out God's judgment from his mission—he is simply adjusting the time-scale. Now, today, for this period of time, this is the day of God's favour and mercy. So let me set you free, give you sight, make you rich. Let me do it now, before it is too late, because judgment is coming. That is what Jesus hints at by leaving out those words from Isaiah, and that is what he makes explicit by showing the way in which God rejects those who reject the salvation he sends them. Now is the day of God's favour, but the day of God's vengeance remains on the horizon.

The penny dropped for me one summer when I was a young boy. As I listened to someone explain why Jesus' message is good news I realised that I was like a prisoner needing to be set free. I realised that I was the one up to my neck in debt before God and that Jesus had come to clear my account. I realised that I was blind and that I wanted to see. I realised that in reading the Bible God was speaking to me directly about my need of a fresh start, of forgiveness and rescue. Since that day I know that I have been welcomed into his family. I've taken my place at the table alongside all the forgiven sinners that we've read about in these pages. My aim in this book has been to show you these things happening to others so that you will ask Christ for mercy and experience the richness of life with him yourself.

Further encounters

Whether you've been in a church for as long as you can remember, or whether you're just curious and would like to know more, the following resources might help. Other books on Jesus like this one include:

- *Christianity Explored*, by Rico Tice and Barry Cooper (Carlisle: Authentic Lifestyle, 2002). An exploration of Jesus' identity and mission from the Gospel of Mark. You can also visit www.christianityexplored.org and find a Christianity Explored course near you.
- *Real Life Jesus*, by Mike Cain (Nottingham: IVP, 2008). A clear and accessible look at the claims of Jesus in John's Gospel.
- *Vintage Jesus: Timeless Answers to Timely Questions*, by Mark Driscoll and Gary Breshears (Wheaton: Crossway Books, 2007). A racy, contemporary presentation of what it is that makes Jesus unique.

If you want to explore the issue of the historical reliability of what you have been reading in Luke's Gospel (or any of the Gospels), then I would recommend:

- *The Da Vinci Code: from Dan Brown's fiction to Mary Magdalene's faith*, by Garry Williams (Ross-shire, CFP, 2006). Whether you've read the book or seen the film, and whether you loved or hated both, Dan Brown expresses the kind of scepticism many have about the truthfulness of the biblical writings. Garry Williams' response is relevant to anyone wanting to examine the evidence. A short and very engaging read.
- *The Historical Reliability of the Gospels*, by Craig Blomberg (Nottingham: IVP, 1987). This book is a much more detailed and scholarly look at each of the four Gospel accounts of Jesus' life.

You may well have other questions about the Christian faith. The following would be worth your time:

- *But is it real? Answering 10 common objections to the Christian faith*, by Amy Orr-Ewing (Nottingham: IVP, 2008); and *What kind of God? Responses to 10 popular accusations*, by Michael Ots (Nottingham: IVP, 2008). Both books tackle hard questions head on and many have found these extremely helpful books.
- *If you could ask God one question*, by Paul Williams and Barry Cooper (Surrey: The Good Book Company, 2007). A well-written look at searching questions.

Other books of Interest from
Christian Focus Publications

SIMON VIBERT

LIVES JESUS **CHANGED**
LESSONS ABOUT LIFE FROM JOHN'S GOSPEL

LIVES JESUS CHANGED
Lessons about Life from John's Gospel
Simon Vibert

If you look at a family album we will begin to get an idea of the events, which have occurred in the life of that particular family. John's Gospel gives a snapshot of Jesus life and the lives he changed. John's gospel tells the story of Jesus the saviour of the world who came in flesh to forgive sins. Simon Vibert invites us to come and see the lives Jesus changed. But all these characters that we meet are not the one that the people had been waiting for. Jesus was that one but all these characters were "signposts" that pointed to Jesus so that might cause us to respond. Ideal for individuals or small group studies.

"John the evangelist was a consummate chronicler and Simon Vibert's book reflects his genius... Vibert shows us how the form is the vehicle that carries the story forward. In fact we feel close to these people and are drawn into their stories."

Paul Wells,
Professor of Systematic Theology,
Facult' Libre Theologie Reformee, Aix-en-Provence, France

"One of the ways in which Matthew, Mark and Luke's Gospels differ from John is that they recount Jesus speaking to crowds, whereas in John, we have many private interviews and conversations. This is the realm that Simon Vibert has marvellously mined in *Lives Jesus Changed*. Quite rightly the emphasis is not so much on the characters themselves but rather at the Lord Jesus and what He was - and is -able to do in numerous lives. Each chapter is very accessible and heart-warming."

Jonathan Fletcher,
Vicar of Emmanuel Church, Wimbledon, London

Simon Vibert is Vice Principal and Director of the School of Preaching at Wycliffe Hall, Oxford.

ISBN 978-1-84550-543-1

RICHARD BEWES

THE TOP

100

QUESTIONS

Biblical Answers to Popular Questions

Plus - Explanations of
50 Difficult Bible Passages

THE TOP 100 QUESTIONS
Biblical Answers to Popular Questions
Richard Bewes

We've all had that sinking feeling when you realise that the question you have just been asked has you stumped. - your mind races to come to a satisfactory answer. Later you kick yourself for not having thought of it and prepared an answer before now. For Christians, when it comes to matters of faith, it can be all the more embarrassing. Christians need to be able to give a reason for their faith, but so often, through our own laziness we fail miserably. As a pastor to a vibrant city church in the heart of London, Richard Bewes faced tricky questions about his faith on almost a daily basis. This book is a compilation of the Top 100 Questions he has been asked by people of all ages, in all walks of life, in various states of religious belief.

The answers Richard offers are not pat answers to outwit the questioner, but rather, he seeks to give clear, biblical advice to genuine questions. This book will help Christians face a sceptical, spiritually curious world.

> "...the accumulated wisdom and illustration from decades of mulling over some very difficult questions - wonderfully distilled down to the key points."
>
> Rico Tice,
> Author, Christianity Explored

> "...gives deeply thought-out, carefully informed answers to many of the questions most troublesome to contemporary humanity."
>
> Dallas Willard,
> Professor of Philosophy, University of Southern California

Richard Bewes was the rector of All Souls, Langham Place in the centre of London for many years. He is an experienced broadcaster, conference speaker and the author of more than twenty books.

ISBN 978-1-85792-680-4

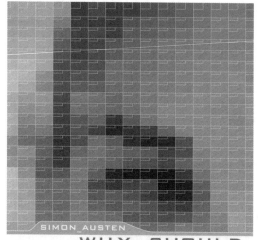

SIMON_AUSTEN

WHY_SHOULD
GOD_BOTHER
WITH_ME?

CHRISTIANITY_FRESHLY_EXPLORED

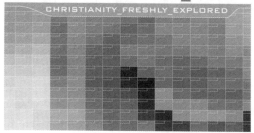

WHY SHOULD GOD BOTHER WITH ME?

Christianity Freshly Explored

Simon Austen

The modern secular viewpoint leaves us insignificant walking monkeys who got a lucky evolutionary break. *Nothing we do matters.* If you are investigating the Christian faith the question 'Why should God bother with me?' is one that needs an answer.

"Shrewd, sane and sensible, I wish this book every success. By success I mean that those who at present don't bother with God will read it and discover that God bothers with them."

Dick Lucas,
Formerly Rector of St Helens Bishopsgate

"An accessible, engaging and comprehensive explanation of the Christian faith, which I thoroughly recommend."

Rico Tice,
Author, Christianity Explored

"Part C.S. Lewis, part John Stott, Austen invites conversation with unbelievers. God has in fact bothered with us more than we know."

Michael Horton,
J. Gresham Machen Professor of Systematic Theolgy & Apologetics,
Westminster Seminary in California, Escondido, California

Simon Austen is Vicar of Houghton and Kingmoor in Carlisle, England

ISBN 978-1-85792-719-1

Christian Focus Publications

publishes books for all ages

Our mission statement –

STAYING FAITHFUL
In dependence upon God we seek to impact the world through literature faithful to His infallible Word, the Bible. Our aim is to ensure that the LORD Jesus Christ is presented as the only hope to obtain forgiveness of sin, live a useful life and look forward to heaven with Him.

REACHING OUT
Christ's last command requires us to reach out to our world with His gospel. We seek to help fulfil that by publishing books that point people towards Jesus and help them develop a Christ-like maturity. We aim to equip all levels of readers for life, work, ministry and mission.

Books in our adult range are published in three imprints.

Christian Focus contains popular works including biographies, commentaries, basic doctrine and Christian living. Our children's books are also published in this imprint.

Mentor focuses on books written at a level suitable for Bible College and seminary students, pastors and other serious readers. The imprint includes commentaries, doctrinal studies, examination of current issues and church history.

Christian Heritage contains classic writings from the past.

Christian Focus Publications Ltd,
Geanies House, Fearn, Ross-shire,
IV20 1TW, Scotland, United Kingdom
info@christianfocus.com
www.christianfocus.com